The Berkeley Book
of College Essays

The Berkeley Book
of College Essays

*Personal Statements for California Universities
and Other Selective Schools*

Compiled by Janet Huseby

Foreword by Ilene Abrams
College Advisor, Berkeley High School

A Cody's Book

Stone Bridge Press • Berkeley, California

Published by
Stone Bridge Press
P. O. Box 8208
Berkeley, CA 94707
TEL 510-524-8732 • sbp@stonebridge.com • www.stonebridge.com

All profits from the sale of this book will go to the Berkeley High School Development Group to support the school's College and Career Center. The first edition of this book was published in 2006 under the title *True Admissions*.

For inquiries, please contact Janet Huseby at jhuseby@pacbell.net.

Cover photo by Mark Coplan, Public Information Officer of the Berkeley Unified School District. The picture was taken at UC Berkeley's Greek Theater during Berkeley High's 2004 graduation.

2012 2011 2010 2009 2008 2007   10 9 8 7 6 5 4 3 2 1

LIBRARY OF CONGRESS CATALOGING-IN-PUBLICATION DATA
The Berkeley book of college essays: personal statements for California universities and other selective schools / compiled by Janet Huseby; foreword by Ilene Abrams.
    p. cm. — (Cody's book)
   ISBN 978-1-933330-60-0 (pbk.)
  1. College applications—United States. 2. Universities and colleges—United States—Admission. 3. Exposition (Rhetoric) I. Huseby, Janet. II. Berkeley High School (Berkeley, Calif.)
LB2351.52.U6B47 2007
378.1'616—dc22
               2007031186

Contents

Getting Started

FOREWORD
By Ilene Abrams, College Advisor, Berkeley High School

Most of the 700 or so seniors at Berkeley High School pass through my door during their senior year. As I get to know them and read their essays, I am often saddened to think that the only audience for their revealing and often heartwarming stories is the admissions committees of colleges around the country. I was very pleased when Janet Huseby proposed publishing a sampling of their essays, because now others can share in the insights and reflections of this thoughtful, diverse group of teenagers.

As you will see from their stories, some live on their own, while others come from well-off families. Some take the bus to school, dropping off brothers and sisters on the way, while their fellow students are driven in SUVs. Some do not have computer or Internet access at home, while the student sitting in the desk next to them meets with a private tutor after school. Yet all are on their way to college, and their stories are compelling. Talking with students as they struggle to find the words to explain what makes them who they are, I realized that the college admissions process in the United States has become like the rites of passage of previous generations all over the world. For these teenagers, it is a time to reflect on younger years and ponder the future, to answer important questions such as, Who am I in the world? How did I get where I am today? What goals do I have for the future? How is my identity defined by what I have done? As part of the process, they complete numerous applications requiring them to fill in their name, address, and Social Security number again and again. Students face up to their grades, reflecting on the work they have done for the previous three years, and make lists of their activities both in and out of school, often thinking about what they've accomplished and what they wish they had done. But it is the college essay that frequently is the most difficult for students, because it is where they try to express the essence of who they are—a difficult task for accomplished writers, let alone students in their late teens.

When I asked some of our alums, a year or more after their high school graduation, for permission to print their personal statement, many told me that they thought their essays were "terrible" or "awful." Yet to me they are a snapshot, taken during the first semester of their senior year, of their vision of who they are, what they have come through, and their hopes for themselves and the world. In that way, they give me hope as well. They show that the vast majority of teenagers do not match the stereotypes depicted on the evening news, but are caring and responsible young people looking to make a better world for themselves and for all of us.

I hope that this book will serve as an inspiration to parents who are struggling with their children during the demanding time of applying to college. And to students trying to keep your heads above water during the first semester of your senior year: Realize that you are not alone. Many others have passed this way before and have matured and grown by using this time to reflect on where they have been and where they want to go.

This is a powerful collection, and not just for the next generation of college applicants and their families. It is a beautiful portrait of a diverse, contentious, and delightful group of young people. They have inherited a world that is often harsh and cruel, but they have found a way to redeem themselves and us with their generosity, perseverance, and heart.

Thanks very much to Janet, whose vision and dedication to this book made it happen. My thanks to her also for always having a smile for me during the busiest and most stressful of times. Thanks also to the essay readers who have come faithfully week after week to help students focus their thoughts and write grammatically, for staying hours after their shifts and for making themselves available to our students through phone and email.

A special thanks to Edna Harris, my partner in the College and Career Center, whose kindness and organization has helped me and the students every day and made our room a safe haven for all.

And thanks especially to the Berkeley High students. You have shared your joys and sorrows and have taught me so much in the process. My life is better for having known you all.

A WORD ON THIS BOOK
By Janet Huseby

If you are about to write a college essay, there is nothing more useful than reading other students' essays. This book is a good place to start: a collection of personal essays for California universities and other selective colleges, written by seniors at Berkeley High School.

The school, which forms a backdrop for many of the essays, is one of a handful of truly diverse high schools in the United States. In 2007, Berkeley had more than 3,300 students: 33.5 percent of the students were white, 29.9 percent African American, 13.1 percent Chicano/Latino, 7.6 percent Asian American, 14.6 of mixed race, and the remainder Filipino, Native American, and Pacific Islander. Approximately 20 percent of Berkeley High students qualified for free or reduced-price lunch, and more than 90 percent of the graduating class planned to attend college.

◆ ◆ ◆

I know Berkeley High well because I have spent the last 11 college application seasons—from late October to the end of November—sitting in the school's College and Career Center from 11:30 a.m. to 12:15 p.m., lunchtime. It is a large, beautiful room with wide wooden tables and college banners tacked on the walls. When the bell rings, the room is wired. Students hustle in to be first in line to talk to Ms. Abrams, the college advisor. Another line forms in front of Ms. Harris, the center's program assistant, who patiently checks packets of transcript requests and recommendation forms. At the essay reader table, students grab chairs to wait their turn for editing and feedback.

I am a writer by trade, with a background in journalism. I started my career at the *Brazil Herald,* as a copy editor writing headlines and proofing the stock quotes. Then I landed a job at the Rio de Janeiro office of the Associated Press, trotting from bombings to Great Train Robber Ronald Biggs's birthday party. By the time I had children, I was freelancing in San Francisco. When my second daughter was writing her college essays, I realized that helping kids with their applications was something I could do. I offered my help to Rory Bled, who was then the Berkeley High college advisor. Next, I took on the task of organizing the 15 or so writers and professionals who faithfully show up for the six hectic weeks that comprise the college application season, coaching students one by one through the most challenging of assignments, the personal essay, in 600 words or less.

◆ ◆ ◆

The season starts slowly, in mid-October. At first, it is almost all girls who show up. In early November, we start to see boys. The last moment is almost all male. Most students start out with a "telling" essay, a flat outline. "Show," we tell them. Why? Where? When? Explain. Describe. Once the details are there, throw out the introduction, scratch the conclusion—if you have told your story convincingly, they are wasted words. The advice is generic, but the goal is a story "only you can tell."

I have learned that essay reading is not so much about the English language as it is about marketing. Here's one essay that wasn't selling: It was about a best friend who was more popular, made better grades, and beat our essay writer out of a place on the varsity team. "I don't know about this," I said. "The colleges are going to want your best friend, not you." Then I found out the rest of the story. The best friend had quit the team and, in the following year, our writer was elected captain. The best part had been left out. "Put it in," I said. Another story: A student dropped out of a competitive sports team and was abandoned by all the teammates she had thought were her close friends. She was devastated, and wrote that the lesson she had learned was not to trust people. "Ouch," I said. "A college doesn't want someone who won't trust anyone." Then we got the rest of the story. Our writer reconnected with her old middle-school friends, and together they began helping at a children's center, a volunteer program that she eventually led. The final draft ended with her sailing past the mean girls out of the gates of Berkeley High, in good company, triumphant.

I have worked with an average of 70 students a year, keeping track of their names on the back of a large manila envelope. Not a year has gone by that I haven't heard of the deaths of at least two parents. One year, I read of two mothers who'd had strokes; another year there were two fathers who committed suicide. I've read essays by an emancipated 16-year-old living on her own in an apartment, and by a girl who drew strength from being looked after by "a large church filled with people wearing beautiful big hats and sharp suits." I've read essays from kids who are gay and from kids who struggle with poverty, taking care of younger siblings and translating for their parents. I loved an essay by one student who was the first in her family aiming for college. She compared taking Advanced Placement classes to visiting a foreign country. First, she explained, "I needed my passport, which was my transcript. Next, I needed to learn a new language." I liked the essay by the student who started out with a sports essay—a generic "no-no" of a topic—and then surprised me by throwing in theater! And I am fond of the student who laid her cards on the table without guile: "When asked to describe myself, I come up with words like 'cheerful,' 'creative,' and 'reliable,'" she writes. "But there is one adjective I usually try to push to the back of my mind in the hope that it will disappear: 'shy.'"

As essay readers, we tell kids there are a couple of basic things to avoid and rules to abide by. Don't preach; don't try to convert; describing hardship works if it ends in redemption; don't feel sorry for yourself, and don't ever complain—especially about having to help your mother, as one boy had the bad grace to do. Don't write about elementary school or even middle school. Watch out for sports essays and travel abroad and camp essays—good ones are hard to write.

One of the tricks college counselors use to help students who are having a hard time figuring out what to write is to jot down a series of chapter titles of their life story and then expand on one of them. For the last 11 years, I have finished every college admission season inspired by the idea of the personal essay and determined to write one of my own. I even have my list of chapters: "On the Boat to Brazil, or My Father the Engineer," "Barnard Blues," "Cub Reporter," and finally, "Sitting by the Sandbox." But, the fact is, I never do finish my own essay, perhaps because writing an essay in 600 words is hard work. Good luck, dear students.

APPLYING TO THE UNIVERSITY OF CALIFORNIA
By Janet Huseby

University of California applications are due at the end of November. Regular Admission deadlines for private colleges range from December 15 to February 15. As a result, most California students who are applying to selective colleges finish their UC essays before other applications.

The UC system does not ask for recommendations from counselors or teachers, which can flesh out and substantiate a student's story. Students are admitted on the basis of their high school classes and grades, test scores, a short list of extracurricular activities, and 1,000 words of their own. The lack of accompanying recommendations gives these essays a special burden. Unlike Common Application essays—used by most private schools and entailing a 500-word essay and a 150-word short answer—UC essays must do more than give the reader a glimpse, however illuminating, into the writer's life. The 1,000 words must cover challenges overcome, passions pursued, summers, family background, and a fleshing out of activities outside the classroom. Think journalism: who, what, when, where, why. In the end, with 1,000 words complete, our applicants should ask: Is this me? Is this everything that is important about me? Have I left anything out? They should also hand the essays to someone who doesn't know them—not a teacher or a counselor or a good friend, but someone who is a stranger, as is the college admissions officer. If the essays work, the stranger will come up with a pleasing list of adjectives to describe our applicant. If the student is not happy with these adjectives, he or she should rewrite.

The UC application asks students to write two essays using a maximum of 1,000 words total. The essays may be of equal length or one may be long and the other short. If you decide to write a long and a short essay, the university suggests your shorter answer be at least 250 words. The official prompts are as follows:

PROMPT #1 (FRESHMAN APPLICANTS)

Describe the world you come from—for example, your family, community, or school—and tell us how your world has shaped your dreams and aspirations.

PROMPT #1 (TRANSFER APPLICANTS)

What is your intended major? Discuss how your interest in the subject developed and describe any experience you have had in the field—such as volunteer work, internships and employment, participation in student organizations and activities—and what you have gained from your involvement.

PROMPT #2 (ALL APPLICANTS)

Tell us about a personal quality, talent, accomplishment, contribution, or experience that is important to you. What about this quality or accomplishment makes you proud and how does it relate to the person you are?

To see what the University has to say on the essays, visit www.universityofcalifornia.edu/admissions/undergrad_adm/apply/how_apply/personal_statement.html.

◆ ◆ ◆

The collection contains six complete sets of UC essays written between 2003 and 2006. Over the years the University of California has consistently required applicants to submit a total of 1,000 words, but the format has varied. Before 2000, students were given three prompts and asked to write their essay on one of them. Between 2001 and 2006, applicants were told to respond to three questions. Now they are being asked to answer two prompts, with the recommendation that if the essays are not of equal length, the shorter one should be no fewer than 250 words. While the format has changed through the years, the task has remained the same: Tell as much about yourself as you can in 1,000 words.

The Essays

Complete UC Essay Packages

While not every student in the section below elected to attend a UC campus, they were all admitted to one or more.

ADRIAN DELMER, a member of the class of 2004 at Berkeley High, is currently a student at UC Santa Cruz.

1. ACADEMIC PREPARATION

I have taken Latin all four years of high school. I chose to take this class in ninth grade because I was interested in the etymology of English words. I soon grew to truly love the class, in large part because of the teacher, Ms. Herndon. I can feel the energy coming from her as she races back and forth across the front of the room, talking about indirect clauses of result and the ablative of absolute. Every day in class she talks about the most interesting Latin facts. For instance, there is truth behind the common myth that a wolf raised the founders of Rome. In the village where they were raised, the word "lupa" meant both wolf and prostitute, and their foster mother slept around quite a bit. I might add that Ms. Herndon expertly covers the required course material.

My hunger for the knowledge that Ms. Herndon piles on us has kept me interested in the language. Even after I failed out of Latin 3 during the first semester of my sophomore year, due to laziness on my part, I retook the class the following year. I have stayed with the class up until now, even though it has proved to be extremely challenging, because I know that it is rare to come across a class this good.

2. POTENTIAL TO CONTRIBUTE

The voice of a 100-year-old violin rings clearly throughout the valley of Camp Wolfeboro in the High Sierra. I, the artist, stand on one of the boulders lining the mountainside. As my playing intensifies, the wind begins to pick up, threatening to cast aside my bow. I persist, playing louder and holding my bow tightly as the horsehairs vibrate in the wind. My fingers fly up and down the neck of the violin, daring the approaching clouds to come closer. But the clouds have brought reinforcements, and a dull rumble emanates from the sky. My fingers speed up with the wind. A bolt of lightning strikes, a chord is struck, a tumultuous roar escapes from the heavens.

Having learned from the Boy Scouts that a high open rock is no place to be during a storm, I decide to put down my violin and give up this battle with the gods. Descending down the mountain, I contemplate my 11-year relationship with music and the violin: one that began when I was six and has taken me from "Twinkle, Twinkle, Little Star" to Tchaikovsky's Concerto in D Major; a relationship that has gotten me to love and play classical, klezmer, blues, jazz, Celtic-fiddle, and bluegrass music; a relationship that has taught me the poignancy of a gypsy tune, the gaiety of an Irish jig, and the beauty of a violin concerto.

My relationship with music has helped me build relationships with people. Over the years, I have played violin in many different settings, both formal and informal. I have played in various quartets and trios at weddings, art shows, and on the street. I was a member of the Young

People's Chamber Orchestra for four years, where I learned the value of leadership and cooperation in musical performance. I found that in order to be a leader, I had to play the violin with confidence. Nobody will follow a person who is afraid to hear the sounds that come out of their own instrument. I eventually became the concertmaster of the orchestra. I have also played in orchestras at Cazadero Music Camp, King Middle School, and Berkeley High School, where I am now the assistant concertmaster.

I have gotten a lot out of music over the last 11 years, but only recently have I started to give back. Every Saturday morning I travel across town to coach students in the Young People's Chamber Orchestra. I also have one private student, a seven-year-old Japanese boy who does not speak any English. Fortunately, music is a language of its own, and I have been able to communicate with my student without the need for words. I teach by demonstration and by waving my arms wildly in the air.

Over the last couple of years I have started to improvise when I practice. I pick up my violin, and instead of walking over to my stand, where pages of Bach and Sarasate await me, I just start to play. Most of my practices begin when I have a certain emotion that I feel can only be expressed through music. This improvisation is not something a teacher has ever taught me to do. It is something I have come to over the years.

Standing high up on the mountainside above Camp Wolfeboro, I sing a song on the violin that has no lyrics; it cannot be written down, it cannot be repeated. I stand on the mountainside and play for anyone in the valley who may hear me. I play for the trees, for the rocks, for the heavens. Mainly, I play for myself.

3. OPEN-ENDED

I did terribly in school during the first semester of tenth grade, and I can blame nobody except myself for the ludicrous grades I received.

The problem was not that I didn't enjoy learning. I loved learning and still do. I just didn't understand that learning was a two-part process: the teacher must teach and the student must take in and process the knowledge.

During the first semester of tenth grade I was willing to let the teachers teach, but I was not willing to do my part. I decided it was easier to lie back on my bed and listen to Pink Floyd than to write an English essay or study for a math test. In other words, I was lazy.

After that semester, I looked back and realized that I had had some of the best teachers Berkeley High had to offer and I hadn't learned a thing. I was very angry with myself for blowing off an opportunity like that. Since sophomore year I have tried my hardest to learn as much as I can in all of my classes, going in during my precious lunch hour and after school to get extra help. My grades reflect this change of heart.

ANDREW GORDON-KIRSCH, class of 2005, attends the University of California at Los Angeles.

1. ACADEMIC PREPARATION

With a ball of clay spinning between my wet fingers, I forget about up-coming calculus and physics exams. All of my energy and dexterity are instead focused on my hands entering the firm gray orb and molding it into a platter for Grandma, mugs for friends, bowls, cups—whatever I feel like making—according to my critical standards. I search for glaze recipes in the Berkeley High book of "potions" that will bring out the very best temmoku black, heino turquoise, or copper shino. For other concoctions, the "secret" ones like deep blues with crystallized white flowers, I hit the chemistry books to determine what compound combinations I need. The ingredients are kept in a locked chamber: not lizard's tooth but rather chrome oxide, feldspar instead of frog's eye. The anticipation of the final product peaks when I look into the small hole on the side of the high-fire kiln and see my piece glowing in the 2,500°F heat. I have a sense of what it should turn out like, but the randomness of the gas pressure within the kiln and human discrepancies in reduction timing leave me, the mad scientist, with an original creation every time!

2. POTENTIAL TO CONTRIBUTE

As I cross the striped white lines on the sticky black pavement into enemy territory, I look up with awe at the mansion in front of me. How could such a fine resort lower itself to maltreating its employees by binding them with a contract that underpays, doesn't provide affordable health care, and denies them unionization? I shake my head with a sigh as I enter the Claremont Hotel through a side door, where they won't expect to find lobbyists like me and my delegation of socially aware teenagers.

"Hi, my name is Andrew. I would like to speak with your manager." I'm the entry man. I get us into the dark depths of administration. The manager of room service tries to plead innocent, saying she has no authority. A finance manager says it's her superiors that are making the bad decisions. Finally, we deliver our message to the restaurant manager. Our tactful push for improved employee contracts receives a canned response. "Thanks for your concern, I'll be happy to call my boss and relay your message to him." Seeing right through his transparent lie, I bring out my cell phone, gesturing for him to take it from my hand. He steps back with a quizzical look. "What are you doing?" "My phone has unlimited weekend minutes," I say. "Feel free to make that call right now." Of course, he refuses, and in no time we are being herded through the main lobby, past the wedding procession, and out the glass doors. Our group made such an impression—a tranquil one, of course—that hotel security escorted us off the premises!

I was at the hotel with Jewish Youth for Community Action (JYCA), a local program, student-created and -led, which has educated and inspired political and cultural awareness in the community and in me. We seek progressive social change through youth empowerment and through taking action in our community. We protest, picket, and lobby. We also give workshops on facilitation, community building, and pressing social issues like homelessness, abortion rights, and the Israel-Palestine conflict.

In addition to helping members of my extended community, I proactively aid members of my immediate community: students at my school. A new student at Berkeley High has it hard. Students from abroad have it three times as hard. Not only are they in a new environment, but the environment doesn't speak their language, nor does it practice the same customs. As chairman of Berkeley High's Ethnic Culture & Language Exchange, I work closely with newly arrived students in the English Learners Department (ELD) to make them feel more at home in the United States and at an American high school of 3,000 students. At least once every month we pair native English speakers with ELD students in an exchange where both sides gain insight on the other's experiences. I facilitate interactive games such as multilingual telephone and "Simon Says." Outside of club meetings, I connect with ELD students by eating lunch with them and showing them around campus. Rodrigo, who had been in America for a week, had questions about English vocabulary—the pronunciations of "through," "thorough," "cough," and similar words that end in "-ough." Delia, from Colombia, wanted to know how government works in America. I tried my best to explain to her the divisions of power and the levels of federalism in simple terms. I made sure to add that America promotes public participation—it's in the Constitution—and that it's up to us activists to ensure that we are headed in the right direction.

3. OPEN-ENDED

Last spring, I took a week off from regular school to work as a cabin leader for fourth- and fifth-graders in the MOSAIC Project, a nonprofit outdoor school run by a woman with an idealistic dream of peace. Our mission is to increase tolerance and to eliminate stereotyping and discrimination by engaging the students in cross-cultural activities and by teaching them nonviolent means of conflict resolution. My cabin won the Cleanest Cabin Award, along with the MOSAIC Award, given to the cabin most exemplifying qualities taught by the MOSAIC Project.

At first it seemed like Jay, Tyrone, and Daniel had nothing in common. Jay is Caucasian, Tyrone is African American, and Daniel is Latino. One lives in Berkeley, one in Oakland, and the other in San Francisco. I'm there to help them get along and become friends. I try to think of a common denominator. "What kind of music do you guys like?" Instantly, a heated debate erupts from my cabin, comparing Snoop Dogg to Kanye West and East- to West-Coast hip-hop. I shout out that I love country music (not true) and that they should all check it out. Silence. Then laughter bursts out as we head up to dinner, our first meal of many as a family of brothers.

CARMELA ZAKON, who graduated from Berkeley High in 2004, is a student at Occidental College in Los Angeles.

1. ACADEMIC PREPARATION

From a young age, I learned to seek out resources to better myself. Being poor, I realize that no one is going to give me a handout. I have to go after my goals in order to improve my circumstances. It is with this mindset that I have pursued my educational aspirations.

My mom did not attend college, so I knew I did not have the option of relying on her to inform me about preparation for college. I had to take the initiative to find a different method. In junior high school, I got involved with the Early Academic Outreach Program. I was enthusiastic to be a member of a support system that could benefit me. I attended weekly meetings where we discussed the preparation necessary in order to become ready for further education. In high school, I became a member of Y-Scholars, another program that assists first-generation college-bound students.

Towards the end of my sophomore year in high school, I received information about a program sponsored by EAOP, in conjunction with UC Berkeley, called the Pre-College Academy. As soon as I learned more about it, I had no doubt in my mind that I would be a part of the Academy. I went though the process of getting teacher recommendations and writing an essay. I was subsequently accepted into the program. I was willing to sacrifice a portion of my summer vacation and forego wages from my job in order to take advantage of this opportunity.

As a student in the Pre-College Academy, I took courses in English Composition, Mathematics, and Psychology. I was enthusiastic—always participating in class discussion and putting a lot of effort into my work. I thrived in the university environment, where self-reliance and dedication is required. I went to my psychology professor's office hours when I wanted to know more about child-development research. I met with the English Teacher's Assistant when I wanted advice to improve my essay on institutionalized power struggles. I had a personal drive to succeed, and had a great time doing it. My hard work paid off in the high quality of my performance, as well as in earning straight As.

As a culmination of the program, there was a presentation of awards. When my name was called as the top student in the Academy, I was taken by surprise. This must be because I never worked for outside recognition: My desire to do my best had been my motivation.

Even though the grades I earned for these courses did not count for credit at my high school, I believe I gained a lot from this experience. I grew not only academically, but interpersonally as well. The self-confidence I developed made it possible for me to get involved in the YMCA's Youth and Government program when I returned to school in the fall. I became coauthor of a mock education bill to set up inner-city students with one-on-one tutoring. This bill was the mock Governor's favorite of our Model Legislature and Court in the State Capitol.

In addition to Youth and Government, this past summer I was a participant in the Summer Law Institute at the UCLA campus. During this weeklong program, I attended lectures of law professors, defended in a mock trial, and met with law students and practicing attorneys. I have come out of each of these experiences stronger and more enthusiastic about continuing to explore my educational aspirations.

2. POTENTIAL TO CONTRIBUTE

Being first-generation college bound gives me a unique outlook and enables me to teach others. In addition, the fact that I am African American and come from a modest upbringing gives me a different perspective from many of my classmates. When we have class discussions, I am able to see situations from a different viewpoint from my peers and voice my opinions. For example, during a discussion in English the other day, a student made the comment that "We all come from middle-class homes." I was quick to raise my hand and offer a different perspective. Unlike my classmate, I know what it is like to not have enough food for dinner, to live in a crowded one-room apartment with my mom and two sisters, and to have the phone service cut off due to unpaid bills. I feel privileged to be able to offer a different perspective on issues that many of the other students cannot relate to. This strengthens the class discussions, because students can view arguments through various lenses. I feel most rewarded when I am able to witness my peers changing their perspective just a bit and saying, "I never looked at it that way before."

3. OPEN-ENDED

My employment positions have helped me develop as a person. At age 14, I began my first job at the Berkeley Unified School District office, through the city of Berkeley Youth Works. I had watched my older sisters attain jobs before me, and I was pleased that it was finally my chance to earn a paycheck.

My duties at the work site consisted of typing, filing, phone operation, and in-person customer service. When I first began, I was somewhat apprehensive about talking to customers and helping them with their concerns. However, as time went by, I found myself beginning to enjoy helping others. I gained confidence in my abilities because I knew that other people were relying on me to do a good job.

Since then, I have moved on to other employment positions at Vista Community College and am currently working at a doctor's office. In each situation, I have taken the knowledge I gained from my first job and added to my skills. Because of my employment, I have not been able to participate in as many extracurricular activities as I would have liked, but I know that I have made good use of my time.

CASEY LAIRD, Berkeley High class of 2007, plans to attend UC Santa Cruz.

1. ACADEMIC PREPARATION

I chose Communication Arts and Sciences (CAS), a small school at Berkeley High, in part because of its emphasis on social justice and community, but also for its media program. I've spent four years in

CAS video classes, where I've learned everything from the particulars of shooting and using camera angles to advanced video editing. Three of the many videos I've done have been featured in the annual Berkeley High Film Festival. The first one was a Public Service Announcement I made as a freshman about drunk driving. The second video I made with a friend in our junior year, starring a bright yellow, vaguely birdish marionette interacting with people. My third movie was a documentary about the local Hyphy Movement at Berkeley High, made with two other CAS students.

Our Hyphy Movement film was also accepted into the young filmmakers section of the Mill Valley Film Festival, one of the biggest international film festivals. We were invited to the screening and got to go on stage and answer questions from the audience. To our surprise, our movie was the featured movie for the youth portion and the entire session was named after our movie.

2. POTENTIAL TO CONTRIBUTE

The first section I turn to in the *San Francisco Chronicle* is Nation and World, usually dominated by Iraq, Afghanistan, and Iran. But occasionally I see an article about Africa, or South America, or Asia, telling of a disaster destroying the homes of thousands of impoverished people, or the latest numbers on disease and illness spreading across the Third World. When I read these articles, images of smiling faces of friends in Shirati, Tanzania, or tentative, nervous smiles from street children selling gum in Morelia, Mexico, come to mind. I read the stories and think about people I've met living in these situations, how their destitute surroundings have dictated their lives, and how the adversities facing them only continue to rise. At the same time, though, these articles leave me frustrated, as they only tell one side of the story.

In the summers before my junior and senior years, I had the chance to go on extended trips abroad—to Morelia, Mexico, for a month and Shirati, Tanzania, for five weeks—through the small school-within-a-school, Communication Arts and Sciences, I attend at Berkeley High. Going to Morelia was the first trip I'd been on without my family, and it was quite a leap of faith for me. The other 10 kids and I lived with Mexican families. We spent our days learning Spanish at an international language school and our evenings helping Mexican college students make videos about social issues facing the city, country, and world.

The following summer, 12 other students, 2 teachers, and I raised more than $30,000 to go to Shirati, Tanzania, a village of about 4,000 on the edge of Lake Victoria, where we taught HIV awareness and helped out at the regional hospital.

Both trips opened my eyes to another world. All my life, I have known that abject poverty existed, but it never seemed real to me. Poverty was a vague concept that was sad, and of course somebody should do something about it, but it never felt real. The people living in the "Third World" were always just numbers that I couldn't attach any real feeling to.

Meeting eight-year-old kids with grimy faces and hands, who spend their entire days selling gum to drivers of passing cars, while I helped make a movie about street kids in Morelia made this poverty real to me. Working in an African hospital where frequent power failures can mean that emergency surgery must be completed by flashlight—or if there are no batteries, the pale glow of a cell phone—brought the reality of the humans experiencing this life every day home to me. Now, reading articles about the spread of cholera or the rise of homelessness brings real faces to mind.

That's only half of the story, however. Newspaper articles make problems like AIDS, hunger, and contaminated water seem insurmountable, impossible to rectify. That's not the case, though, I now know. Small-scale, incremental efforts do make a difference, and small, dedicated groups can help to better lives in the Third World. One group of students or teachers may not be able to stop the spread of disease in Africa, but we did replace the damaged and missing mosquito screens in the hospital, so that newborn babies won't be attacked by mosquitoes and infected with malaria. We can come home with a plan to raise more money to provide a generator for the hospital, so patients can have reliable electricity. As an individual I can make small, positive changes that will make a big difference in the lives of other people.

3. OPEN-ENDED

The first time I heard the blues was in ninth grade. The song was a stomping, instrumental, Texas-style shuffle called "Hideaway," by the immortal Freddie King, featuring his dazzling, singing guitar front and center for all of two-and-a-half minutes. I was sitting on a stool in the musty room above Subway Guitar Shop with my guitar teacher Kerry when he told me he had something he thought I'd like and popped it in his CD player. I'd been playing electric guitar and taking lessons from Kerry every week for a year and a half, but that was the first playing that really knocked me on my butt. That night I went home and stayed up past midnight learning the entire song note for note, which I can still play to this day, exactly along with the record.

From the down-home Texas Blues of Freddie King, to the funky R&B of King Curtis and the classic Motown recordings of Smokey Robinson, to home-grown country like Hank Williams, my guitar has led me to a wide love of music and a continued drive to continue to explore the great lexicon of American music.

LUCIEN KAHN is a member of the BHS class of 2007. He plans to attend Vassar College.

1. ACADEMIC PREPARATION

Huge rectangles of light pour through the tall windows of UC Berkeley's Pauley Ballroom. Tables numbered 1 to 100 are lined up in perfect rows throughout the hushed hall. Some have been deserted; at others, opponents still struggle as time clicks away. Staring at the white and black pieces on the board before me, I imagine a sequence of moves as seconds fall on the electronic screen at the edge of my board. I calculate each move twice to make sure I see all of the possibilities. "There are as many possible chess positions as there are atoms in the universe," I remember my chess teacher, Robert, telling me.

Across from me, my opponent, an old man with thin white hair, intently watches the board as if the miniature armies had come to life. When I am finally satisfied with my analysis, I grasp the white bishop and slide it across the board along its diagonal. I tap the button on top of the clock, stopping my timer and starting his. We have been concentrating for over three hours and his timer is counting down the final 45 minutes.

My dad taught me to play chess when I was six years old, and I began taking lessons at school. Over the years, I started a chess club at my middle school, gave chess lessons, organized a tournament, and worked as a paid tournament director. At Berkeley High I continued to play, both on the school team and in adult tournaments. As I became more and more serious about playing chess, I got up early each morning and set a timer for 15 minutes to study chess from Polgar's collection of over 5,000 chess problems. I have also researched the history and development of chess from its origins in ancient India. Because of my interest in glass-blowing, I decided to make a chess set out of glass, designing scale drawings for each piece and spending a day in an artist's glass studio to create them. The game ranks up there with my two other favorite sports, baseball and crew. Chess is incredibly complex, but beautifully simple when played well.

The old man moves his knight and hits the clock. Quiet, intense concentration returns. I sharpen my focus on the board to see how his move has changed my options. More space on the king side, and my bishops are far more active than his pieces. If I can maneuver my knight and bishop to put pressure on his castle, I can create an attack he cannot defend. My plan may not work, but it's worth a shot. I lift my knight to an intimidating black square near his castled king and tap the clock.

To me, chess is not just a game, it is an art. When I study a master's game I appreciate the strategic organization of the pieces and the economy of each move. Because there are so many options in chess, there are many opportunities to make a mistake. But I learned that mistakes are part of playing chess. "To become a chess master you must win a thousand games," Robert taught me. "But more importantly, you must lose a thousand games." When I learned that my mistakes are opportunities to improve as a chess player, I wasn't afraid of losing. I've taken this philosophy into other aspects of my life, as well, such as rowing and academics. In chess and in life I have found that I can always learn from my mistakes, but I can't succeed unless I am willing to put my pieces on the board and take risks.

2. POTENTIAL TO CONTRIBUTE

My mom, dad, pets, and I have lived in the same house for all 17 years of my life. I love our old house, even if it is simple and lacks a few appliances. My mom and I cook popcorn the old-fashioned, stovetop way because we have no microwave. When it is time to clear the table, I wipe scraps into the compost; we have no garbage disposal—my dad says they are bad for the environment. And the dishes must be washed by hand because, to my friends' horror, we have no dishwasher. "How do you do it?" they ask me.

"Well . . . soap," I tell them.

Our house does have one room that few others have. Downstairs, behind a sliding wooden door, is my dad's darkroom. I remember helping him develop photographs when I was in elementary school. Just before the image began to emerge, he told me to say "Abracadabra." I was convinced that the magic word made the picture appear. Now I know that the magic is not in the word, or even the chemistry. True magic is finding beauty through patience, skill, and hard work.

My parents have taught me that how people live is more important than what they own, that creating is better than consuming, and that magic can be found in discovery and exploration.

3. OPEN-ENDED

Someone once asked me what my guiding philosophy was. I didn't know what to say at first. I knew it would have to have alliteration, one of my favorite figures of speech, and be funny but meaningful. The motto I came up with was: "Mayonnaise in Moderation." For me, "Mayonnaise in Moderation" sums up how I can be happy in life. "Life is just like a sandwich," I explain to my skeptical peers. "Not enough mayo and it's too dry; too much and it falls apart."

"What does that even have to do with life?" a friend objects.

"Well, putting mayonnaise on a sandwich is like taking risks in life."

As a kid I erred mostly on the safe side, spreading the thinnest layer of mayonnaise I could possibly apply. As I grew and matured I found that if I took an extra risk here and there, rewards awaited my gamble. During winter break of my sophomore year I took an opportunity I previously would have been too frightened to accept: I rowed out beyond the Golden Gate Bridge, alone, in a single scull. That day the mayonnaise was thick and the sandwich was almost falling apart, battered by waves. But sometimes a sandwich like that tastes just right.

NAT SMITH graduated from Berkeley High in 2005.
He is currently a student at Dartmouth College.

1. ACADEMIC PREPARATION

During my junior year, French class became more than just exercises and grammar—we started to translate. We translated children's books, poetry, operas, and classic French literature. My favorite story that we translated was *The Count of Monte Cristo*. Our French version was abridged and illustrated; nevertheless, it caught my interest. After everyone turned his or her book in, I kept going. I went and purchased a copy of the unabridged translation, and read all 1,276 pages over the period of a month. Reading the English version (as opposed to the French) gave me insight into how translators and editors work. For me, reading *The Count of Monte Cristo* helped me realize that studying French was not just for finishing requirements in order to graduate but learning how to communicate with another culture. *The Count of Monte Cristo* gave depth to France, the French language, and the French culture for me, not to mention it is an awesome story.

2. POTENTIAL TO CONTRIBUTE

I like organizing groups of people together to do fun things. During my junior year, my friends and I organized an unofficial "capture-the-flag" club in a Berkeley park, which sponsored a series of well-attended games. Later in the year, capture-the-flag turned into softball. Over the summer I went on an Ocean Classroom course at sea. To the delight of the rest of the crew, I found myself in the enjoyable role of organizing my watch into interpretive dances instead of the run-of-the-mill ship-wide navigation meetings.

At Berkeley High, I am one of the water polo leaders, both in the water and out. As co-captain, I lead the daily dry-land workouts (a practice I instituted), hold team meetings when the coach is too flabbergasted to talk with us, and lead the team in its signature gutter-yell before every game. My team is part of a league in the foggier part of the San Francisco Bay Area. The tournament games pit us against kids who live in the sunny parts, where they swim and play year-round. The result is a lot of disappointing losses. I have my work cut out to maintain our scrappy, happy-go-lucky attitude, which I do by encouraging, joking, and consoling when necessary.

The water polo season is over, and lacrosse has not yet started, but it might be time to start the kick-the-can league.

3. OPEN-ENDED

My Saturday mornings have always been spent in bed with a book, most likely one I fell asleep reading the night before. All of my life what I've read has made an impression on me. Books have given me the key to experience the world as I do. One thread has been a love of the sea and the heroes that come with it.

I received the *Hornblower* series in the second grade; true, my mother read the books to me. I followed Captain Hornblower with the *Howard Pease* series—tramp steamers, third mate Todd Moran, mysteries in the depths of the South Pacific, and the fog-shrouded wharves of Depression-era San Francisco. Then came 23 books in the *Alexander Kent* series, following Richard Bolitho in the British Navy through the American Revolution and the Napoleonic Wars. I realized all these early heroes of mine believed one thing: "Life is an adventure—say yes to it and see where you go."

And they were right. Following this heroic thread in my own life, I can trace learning to sail in elementary school as part of a flotilla of dinghies braving the elements of the San Francisco Bay, to competing in my Laser off the coast of San Diego, to a Naval Academy summer seminar living the life of a plebe (to the puzzlement of my Berkeley friends), and finally, this summer, a 40-day Outward Bound tall-ship sailing course, climbing the mast to furl sails, standing watch all hours, navigating amongst commercial shipping, and diving into the frigid waters of Nova Scotia for Outward Bound's dual swim test and bathing session.

Just as my heroes promised, while I sailed the northern Atlantic I met adventure. Hit with an attack of appendicitis, I was helped by sailors of the French Coast Guard to balance and jump from ship to ship in a rainstorm, where a volunteer French doctor holding a rusty knife greeted me by mimicking surgery—his idea of a joke. The Coasties took me to St. Pierre et Miquelon, a small French island off the Newfoundland coast, where I spent the night undergoing an emergency appendectomy. Under the influence of morphine, I found I was fluent in French, which was fortunate as no one spoke English. The hospital had one phone, which I used to have money wired to me so I could pay for the fine services of the island surgeon and to purchase passage on a small plane that flew out twice a week. I spent four days in that hospital listening to the whispers in French, "*C'est le type du bâteau*"—the guy from the boat. After being discharged I flew to St. John's, where I met the ship that had left me stranded five days earlier. The ship, however, sailed on without me, and I was left to experience my Outward Bound solo in a Maritime hotel—complete with room service—while I recovered from the operation. As I hobbled around St. John's, tender of stomach, I kept in mind how my heroes would have handled themselves: with courage and good cheer. With that in mind, I set off to find a good bookstore.

SAM LYON graduated from Berkeley High in 2007. He plans to attend UC San Diego.

1. ACADEMIC PREPARATION

I have always liked problem-solving. The idea that numbers indicate how fast to thrust a jet or how powerfully to shock a spastic heart to restore it to its natural rhythm fascinates me. Last year, however, I discovered that math problems are broader than numbers—they encompass motivation and understanding as well.

My sophomore year, I had an inexperienced math teacher. I almost never rely on, or even use, the textbook for a class, because I find textbooks more confusing and less interesting than teachers. This time, however, I was forced to decipher the strange examples and pictures in my textbook to glean the formulas I needed. The book put up a fight, but failed to prove itself worse than my teacher.

Junior year, to my dismay, I discovered that a good friend of mine had the same textbook. Since we often did our homework together, I attempted to explain the book to him. Teaching my friend forced me to assume a different perspective: Instead of just trying to figure out how I could solve a given problem, I had to figure out a way to show him how to solve it. I realized very quickly that my friend just did not see the symphony of numbers I saw when I solved a problem. My solution was to give my friend the tools and step back. Instead of forcing him to approach math problems the same way I did, I merely substituted my own drawings for confusing ones in the textbook, and gave the concept explanations the textbook lacked altogether. With this boost my friend began doing problems successfully his own way.

That same year I learned that math problems could include not only understanding but motivation as well. In my junior year I helped create Partnerships for Success, a Berkeley High program, which pairs students in remedial or otherwise decelerated math classes with students in advanced math courses for a year-long tutoring partnership. I worked with a sophomore geometry student. Initially, I assumed her bad grades meant she didn't care about school. I braced myself for a year of conflicting values and low effort. However, it took me little time to realize that she did care. She was cheerful, interested in the material, and never seemed reluctant when we were scheduling our next session. I couldn't understand why she was failing geometry.

Abruptly, one day she informed me that her friends thought she should drop out of school. They had pointed to her low grades and essentially asked her: Why bother? For me, raised to eat, sleep, and drink college, hearing this was dumbfounding. From that point on, my tutoring role became two-pronged: math and motivation.

Every Tuesday and Thursday we met in our math classroom for an hour. She often said "I'm so stupid!" whenever she made a mistake, no matter how small. One day I stopped her mid-phrase, looked straight into her eyes, and said, "Don't say that. Both of us know you're smart." She looked at me for what felt like a very long moment, during which I'm sure my cheeks turned red, before nodding and returning her eyes to her paper, scanning for her error.

As the year progressed, so did her grades. Finally, in May, she showed me a B-plus she'd earned on a unit test. The grade reflected her hard work, but I felt as if maybe a very, very small slice of the cake had my name written on it.

2. POTENTIAL TO CONTRIBUTE

My eyelids creak open and I glance at my alarm clock. It reads 11 a.m. Remembering to guard my language, I yell "Shoot!" and jump out of bed, only to remember I am not a counselor anymore.

Transitioning back from sleep-away camp counselor to student was difficult. On mornings such as this one, I find it hard to believe that there are not 12-year-olds waiting to be woken up, reminded to shower, and shepherded to breakfast.

I miss the individuality of my campers. Whenever I planned an activity I had to remember that while Jeremy, Justin, and Noah loved sports, Jonah and Adam liked art, and Sam needed a leg-up in any program's social aspects. My greatest achievement of the nine-week summer was an activity for my kids that combined sumo wrestling, a fireside chips and salsa party, and male-bonding stargazing.

I never imagined the feeling of being there for a camper in need. Whenever I treated a scrape, sat with a sick camper, or helped another work with his autism, I was filled with feelings of devotion too powerful to describe.

They say there is no greater joy than working with children; this summer proved that to me.

3. OPEN-ENDED

I represent Berkeley's Congregation Beth Israel on the West Coast regional board of NCSY, the National Conference of Synagogue Youth. I first became involved after attending a convention in Los Angeles with some friends a few years ago. We rushed back to start our own NCSY chapter in Berkeley.

Our chapter aims to help teens bond, form a community, and develop a strong sense of Jewish identity. Most of our events are social, but every event has educational content. Recently we held a weekend retreat with 40 people, which alternated between fun activities (stand-up comedy, laser tag) and serious discussion about being proactive (visiting the elderly and giving bag lunches to the homeless were the two favorite suggestions).

As a member of the chapter board in my sophomore and junior years, I attended the yearly NCSY leadership seminar in Los Angeles, where I learned rules for leading a successful team. This year, as a regional board member, I led the team running the same seminar. As I had learned, I worked at the level of, not above, my team; I kept my whole team completely informed, and I kept a positive attitude. My team led the seminar without a hitch.

The Short Essay: 150 to 200 Words

Both the UC application and the Common Application ask for short essays, either 150 or 200 words long. Writing a short essay can be compared to composing a poem—every word counts. But, despite their abbreviated length, a great deal can be said.

Baily Hopkins, a member of the class of 2004, attends UC San Diego.

I live in Berkeley, California; I am a girl and a card-carrying member of the Boy Scouts of America. I started out in the Girl Scouts in first grade, but wasn't excited by the knitting and cookie sales. So, in middle school I switched allegiance to Venturing, a co-ed section of the Boy Scouts. Less than two months into being a Boy Scout, I was off backpacking at the High Adventure Philmont Scout Ranch in New Mexico. In 2002, I was one of the first two girls from the United States to take part in the Central American Camporee in Panama. For the next Central American Camporee, happening this January 2004 in Nicaragua, I have been elected the Patrol Leader, the scout chosen to lead all American Scouts attending the camporee.

My Venture crew is one of two scouting crews to publicly make a stand against the Boy Scouts' anti-gay policy. In February 2003 we issued a public statement that we wouldn't discriminate against anyone because of his or her sexual orientation. We knowingly risked getting kicked out of scouting and stripped of our medals. The organization Scouting for All awarded us rainbow knots to wear on our uniforms and serve as a constant reminder of our belief in doing what's right. I am honored to be a scout.

JULIA BRADY is a member of the BHS class of 2007. She plans to attend Bryn Mawr.

I hadn't even left the Paris airport and I was already faced with a task worthy of a low-budget '70s game show. The Challenge: Find cream for my coffee. The Catch: No one speaks English. The flashy host in his polyester suit smirks, thinking he's given me an impossible task. But what he doesn't know is that I have Berkeley High French under my belt. I boldly go up to the café counter and in my very best French ask for some cream. The waitress smiles and a pitcher of cream appears. The crowd goes wild, "We have a winner!" shouts Ed McMahon, a duck descends, and I walk away overjoyed at my success. At that moment, all the long, arduous hours of French translation and the nerve-wracking speeches in front of my class seem worth it. My victory, though it may appear small, was an epiphany, a realization that I had the ability to speak another language. And it felt GOOD.

French is just the beginning; three times a week I drag myself out of bed, bleary-eyed but eager, for a 7:30 a.m. extracurricular Italian class. This past summer I spent nearly two months in Italy, traveling and living with a family, immersed in Italian life. My host father and I would sit outside on hot summer nights eating plums from his organic farm. We would shuffle through discussions on the Slow Food Movement and the role of immigrant workers in California and Italy, often diving for the dictionary to look up *orto* (kitchen garden) or "watershed" (*spartiacque*).

For me, languages are a ticket to the knowledge the world has to offer, and I hope to learn as many as possible. And next time, I'll ask for a croissant too.

MEHMET SEFLEK, a member of the Berkeley High class of 2005, attends UC Berkeley.

STANFORD UNIVERSITY PROMPT

Jot a note to your future roommate relating a personal experience that reveals something about you.

Hey Jake,

I won't be able to eat lunch with you at Brannan Dining Hall, but I promise, I'll buy you lunch tomorrow to make up for it. If you're wondering why, my parents are coming to check out the campus for a little while, and I have to be their tour guide. You should've heard my dad on the phone, he was so happy for me. I don't know if I told you this, but neither my dad nor my mom went further than middle school, so having their son be the first in the family to study at a university is thrilling for them. It's almost as if they are the ones researching cell fate with Professor Bergmann, learning the intricacies of genomes in Bio 118, or organizing potlucks for the Islamic Society of Stanford University.

Anyway, we're going to be near the Science and Engineering Quad, so you just might get a chance to meet them when you get out of class. Talk to you later.

NINA GORDON-KIRSCH, a member of the Berkeley High class of 2007, is deferring her enrollment at the University of Southern California for a yearlong community service project based in Israel that includes travel to Portugal, Uganda, South Africa, and India.

I believe practicing social justice does not preclude having a good time. I do a variety of volunteer work, but my favorite "make a difference" activity has been the "Clothes Swaps" that I organized and implemented. After the Asian tsunami of 2004, I set out to run a clothing drive and realized I could make it an opportunity to socialize as well as provide help to the victims. As a girl of action, I typed up flyers and handed them out at school. The flyers drew more than 30 girls to my house carrying bags of clothes: jeans, fancy dresses, tank tops, T-shirts, sweatshirts, and shoes. Girl after girl came through my front door, helped themselves to refreshments, and proceeded to try on clothes. I instructed each donor to keep five items, and then we folded the rest into 20 large brown boxes. The swap was such a huge success that I decided to make it an annual event. Over the years I've donated to the tsunami relief, poor children in Brazil, and Katrina relief. However, this fall I wanted to help out in my local community, so I brought the clothes to YEAH (Youth Emergency Assistance Hostel), a youth shelter in Berkeley.

The Long Essay: 500 Words or More

With a few exceptions, most private schools now use the Common Application, which asks for a 500-word essay and a 150-word short answer. In addition, many private schools round out the Common App with supplementary questions. California students usually end up reworking their UC application for the Common Application. And, usually, distilling an essay from 600 words to 500 improves it considerably. In fact, the improvement is so great that I always suggest writing double and then simmering down by half—no matter what length is called for.

Most of the following essays are either the 500-word Common App essay or the 600-word long UC essay. In the cases where the essay is responding to a supplementary question, I have included the question. Every essay in this collection was written by a Berkeley High senior for his or her college application.

AARON MAZEL-GEE graduated from Berkeley High in 2005 and is currently a student at Brown University.

With considerable curiosity, uncertainty, and apprehension, I decided to embark on a five-week "language and culture exchange" in China last summer. As one of 30 American students living at a Beijing university, I'd explore the history, language, and culture of a side of me I had thus far ignored.

I felt anxious about my decision to go to China. Having never closely connected with my Chinese heritage, I worried that I would scarcely belong. My experiences growing up were different from those of the few Chinese kids I'd known. As the child of a white Jewish mother and Chinese father, I've come to recognize that growing up biracial is an enormous asset, but I didn't always feel this way. For a long time I found myself forced to straddle cultures, never able to call one country my ancestral homeland. There rarely were family gatherings of the sort my single-cultured friends enjoyed, where both sides—at least temporarily—become one. Not only are the two sides of my family separated by different customs and interests, they don't even share a common language.

At first, I sensed the need to choose one side or the other, as if they were baseball teams squaring off. To my father's disappointment, I connected much more with my mother's side. I went to a Jewish preschool and later an extracurricular religious school, all of which culminated in my bar mitzvah. After that, I joined two Jewish high school programs.

Almost as an afterthought, I attended a Sunday Chinese school during third and fourth grades. I never made many friends there, however, and because of soccer practice, piano lessons, and religious school, Chinese school fell by the wayside. Almost all my friends were Jewish, and our common culture bound us. I never formed such lasting connections with Chinese friends or customs, besides the occasional Chinese New Year's family banquet or the money-filled red envelopes traditionally given by Chinese grandparents.

On the trip, however, I realized that I do belong. I identified with many more aspects of Chinese life than I had ever expected. Standing on the Great Wall, I could look back into history to see my ancestors building it. Watching Shaolin monks practice martial arts, I was reminded of the martial arts classes that comprised the "cultural" aspect of my Chinese school, one of my favorite parts. The food was similar to the food I ate at home, and the people looked similar to half of my extended family.

The greatest surprise, however, was that I fit in with the other students. Although I wasn't fully Chinese, I felt as much a part of the group as the others. We all shared a common tie—an interest in our heritage. No matter how we had been raised, we were all connected to this vast country and its history.

As a result of this special opportunity to submerge myself in Chinese culture, I feel liberated and more comfortable with my Chinese roots. I have deepened the connections with my Chinese relatives and no longer feel the need to shy away from that part of my background. The discussions of Chinese American identity that my father often encourages have taken on new meaning for me. Living in China has taught me how important it is to challenge myself in order to broaden my personality and sense of self.

ABIGAIL SMITH graduated from Berkeley High School in 1994, from Dartmouth College in 1998, and from Tuck Business School in 2005. Between college and business school, she returned to Berkeley High to teach math. Among her students were several who appear later in this collection. Below is her Dartmouth College essay, which she wrote as a Berkeley High senior.

"She's OUT!" I yell in my best umpire voice. I stand up slowly, stretching to my full five-feet, one-inch, daring anyone to question me. The game is over, Dr. Brennan's Smile Makers winning by a whopping 24 to 16.

I never feel more lonely than when I'm standing in the middle of a baseball diamond wearing my bright yellow umpire's jacket. Unlike the players, I do not have a coach, teammates, or parents on my side. It's my job to call the plays, keep track of the outs, and make sure each girl gets enough playing time. I must make sure that the coaches are respecting the players, the parents are respecting the coaches, and that I'm conducting myself in such a way that everyone respects me. The league in which I'm an umpire is a girls' softball league for second- to fifth-graders. Its purpose is to teach the girls how to play softball, but more important, how to play on a team. What I've found most challenging, though, is dealing with parents and coaches who become impatient watching the game, which is full of bungled plays. They often take their frustration out on the umpire.

When I started umpiring three years ago, I had a hard time dealing with angry coaches and parents. Just as the players were learning to play softball, I was learning to be an umpire. As time went on, not only did I get to know the rules better, but I learned to hold my hands up and yell out, "Dead ball!" knowing that I was right. I learned to listen to the coaches when they complained and then to tell them, calmly, that my call would stand. I learned that when I did make a bad call, I had to put it behind me; I could not let myself get shaken up. I learned that looking straight into the coaches' eyes would make them realize that I couldn't be pushed around.

My favorite time is when a girl gets up to bat and just slams it, way out there. I love the sight of the coaches frantically waving the runners on and the teammates lining up to congratulate the usually astounded batter. As a graduate of the league, I remember the thrill I felt when I reached home plate. But I also remember watching the umpires and wanting to be one. In a girls' league, where most of the coaches are men,

I feel that it is important for the girls to see me in a position of authority.

Because umpiring is such a lonely job, I've had to become my own coach and my own teammates. Just as the coaches tell their girls, "Good job out there," I always congratulate myself after a call. I have gotten some strange looks from players as I walk back to my favorite position between first and second, saying out loud, "Good call, ump, keep it up!"

Over the years I have gained a reputation in the league. The coaches know that I'm fair, they know that I'm doing my best, and they know that I'm having fun. In my first year of umpiring, coaches contested my calls because they knew that with a little bullying, I would back down. They don't even try anymore.

The game is over, the players are eating their snacks, and the parents are picking up discarded mitts. I regretfully take off my yellow umpire jacket and return it to the head coach of Dr. Brennan's Smile Makers. He smiles at me and cheerfully signs my umpire payment card. Now I have to make the long trek across the diamond into the dugout of the losing team, Chez Panisse. Silence falls over the crowd as I present my payment card to be signed. The coach grimly takes my card and signs it. As I reach for it, he shakes my hand. Then, smiling, he says deliberately, "Good game, ump."

ANONYMOUS

She went for a walk and didn't come back. In one split second, a driver took my mom's life and shattered my family. And as I grappled with the horror of this terrifying reality, she wasn't there to comfort me. She was gone. As a nine-year-old, I had to figure out the pain on my own.

My dad had his own grief. He had lost his wife of 23 years, and with her went the life he had always known. He was devastated; unsure of how to pick up the pieces of our family. He didn't know how to deal with my pain, how to comfort a child who missed her mom. And he still doesn't.

After eight years as a single parent, he has yet to assume the fatherly role I long for him to take. Our interactions are superficial—he works, I go to school, he gets home, I do homework. We don't discuss the world or politics, or his life or mine. There's no mention of his job, my classes, or a funny story. If I'm frustrated, I can't talk to him about it. If I'm sad, he's not there to give me a hug. He works so hard to provide for us, but he can't provide the emotional support I need most. So I take care of myself.

I buy the groceries so there's food in the refrigerator. I wash my clothes so they don't sit in the basket. I do the things I see my friends' parents do for them, like filling out school forms or obtaining a parking permit. My dad doesn't want any part of the family dinners that I so crave and want to re-create, so I cook for myself, or sometimes end up eating cold cereal in my room, accompanied by my physics book. I've learned that tears don't help. No matter how hard I try to make our relationship deeper, it doesn't change.

But what I can't get from my dad, I get from my friends, both young and old. My friends are always there for me and love me unconditionally. These are the people who support me when I've had a rough day and who are proud of me when I win a school election. They come to my dance performances and field hockey games, and they bring me soup when I'm sick. They are my true family, the one that my dad can't quite figure out how to create. With them, my life is rich, joyful, and meaningful.

My mom is gone, there's nothing I can do to change that. I've almost come to accept it. But I maintain hope for me and my dad. There's a chance we haven't lost it all. I'll be ready for the day when my dad decides to be the father I long for, but until then, I'll continue to develop independence and enjoy the rich relationships I have with my friends.

ARI ROKEACH graduated from Berkeley High in 2007. He plans to attend UC Davis.

Among my teachers, I'm known as Ari Rokeach. But to my friends, I'm also known as torriealba@yahoo.com. This email handle (albeit with a twist on the spelling) is a tribute to my favorite baseball player, Yorvit Torrealba, a former catcher for the San Francisco Giants who never received the recognition he deserved. And it gives a clue about who I am: an avid player of fantasy sports who can spot talent a mile away.

My older cousin Josh introduced me to fantasy baseball one weekend when I was in ninth grade. He explained how each manager drafts a team of players from Major League Baseball, applying the players' real-life stats to the fantasy team as he competes against other managers in the league. The fantasy manager adds, drops, and trades players, scouting just as in real baseball. Mesmerized by his explanation, I promptly enrolled in his league.

But I didn't stop there. I took it upon myself to be a fantasy baseball ambassador, creating my own league and inviting nine of my friends to join, along with my younger brother, Zach, who was still in junior high.

Fantasy baseball was unlike anything I had ever done before. Suddenly, I was the manager of my very own baseball team. Not only that, I was the commissioner of a league, with 10 teams under my influence. I determined which player stats would count, how many pitchers and hitters could be on each team's roster, and a nominal entry fee.

My fascination with fantasy baseball expanded into other sports as their seasons rolled around, first fantasy football, and then fantasy basketball. Now in my fourth year of fantasy sports—as both a team manager and a league commissioner—I've mastered the art of sniffing out up-and-coming players and measuring the worth of aging superstars. About a month before a draft, I begin to comb through the Yahoo and ESPN sites, reading experts' articles about various players' potential.

Then, I cross-reference the projections with how the players have performed in past seasons to come up with my list of top picks for the draft.

When I started AP Statistics this fall, it was with a leg up: I already had exposure to real-world applications of statistical analysis. And, thanks to my daily dose of the San Francisco Chronicle's sports pages and the various sports news Websites, I've picked up the lingo of sports writing. In the spring of my junior year, I decided to put that new language to work by writing a series of sports articles for Berkeley High's Jacket newspaper, graduating this fall to my own column dedicated to professional sports.

After herding my friends through all the complex steps of drafting and managing their fantasy teams, and mediating the many disputes that come with the league commissioner territory, the role of co-captain of the men's varsity water polo team at Berkeley High this fall came easily to me. I walked the line between drill sergeant and cheerleader, guiding 15 brawny guys in grueling dry-land warm-ups and helping to lead the varsity team to its first league championship title in five years.

Most important of all, fantasy sports have brought me closer to the people in my life, and especially to the person who sits a couple of feet away from me every night, my brother, Zach. As we sit back-to-back while facing our computer screens and traveling through the virtual world of fantasy sports, we trade tips about players and bounce our planned trades off each other. The more we connect and bond over our shared passion, the more the age difference between us disappears.

ARIANNA TABOADA, Berkeley High class of 2006, is a student at UCLA.

As I stepped onto the stage, tightly gripping the microphone, I inhaled deeply and took my place at the small X marked in the middle of the stage. The curtain came up and without hesitation I began to speak. "*Buenas noches, cómo están?*" The crowd cheered in response, and I quickly repeated myself in English, "Good evening, how is everyone doing tonight?" The response was equally deafening. I had emceed three years now for En Pointe Youth Dance Company. "For those of you who aren't familiar with En Pointe, we are a youth dance company from California, founded by two Berkeley teenagers when they were in the seventh grade." Well, no one was familiar with En Pointe in this town; we were in the middle of what is known as colonial Mexico.

I proceeded with my introduction, first in Spanish, then in English. "Everything, from lighting and sound, choreography and costumes, fund-raising and, of course, dancing, is run by youth." My position with En Pointe had grown over the years, from usher, to emcee, to spokes-woman. My involvement grew each year, and this year, as we took on our latest artistic endeavor, I became the public relations manager. Honestly, this title doesn't accurately describe my role. I was simply helping carry out a dream that had been born a year earlier, when one of my best friends came to visit me in Mexico: bringing a group of Berkeley dancers to Mexico to participate in a dance and cultural exchange.

Like many first-generation Mexican Americans, I grew up speaking both Spanish and English. My parents attended higher education in the United States and fully understand and support the importance of both English fluency and maintenance of native language, but it is a challenge in American culture. My parents worked to enforce the rule of "English at school, Spanish at home." At the dinner table, it was Spanish only; if we asked for the bread to be passed, no one passed the basket until we asked in Spanish. Never having been enrolled in formal Spanish-language classes, our vocabulary was limited in certain areas. There were times when my sisters and I began to speak in Spanglish to each other, which my parents absolutely forbade, fearing it would corrupt both our languages. We would have conversations about school, work, even boring things like computers, all in Spanish, in order to increase our vocabulary. It is a problem for many Mexican-origin families to squeeze Spanish into an English-dominated society, but luckily, my family had the resources to do everything possible for me to maintain a bilingual identity. Sophomore year, my mother was offered a job at La Universidad Autónoma de Querétaro in central Mexico. My experience at a private Mexican high school was very different than my year at a large urban American public high school had been. At Berkeley High, I was considered too light-skinned, too green-eyed, too studious even, to possibly be Mexican American. I remember being asked to read aloud in Spanish class, and looking up to my classmates staring at me, thinking, "Where did that white girl learn that Spanish!" In Mexico, I was accepted for who I was: a light-skinned, green-eyed, bilingual Mexican American with college-educated parents. No one did a double-take when I spoke Spanish; in fact, it was the opposite: everyone wanted to know where I had learned English so well. I have had the opportunity that most Mexican Americans will never have: exposure to a high academic level of Spanish. I read books, wrote papers, even won a public speaking award in a language I had once only associated with talking. As a result, I am able to articulate myself both orally and academically to a very wide variety of people.

This certainly came in handy the summer En Pointe traveled to Mexico to participate in a dance and cultural exchange. I was in charge of making arrangements with hotels, language schools, and rehearsal space for the twelve dancers and six parents, as well as putting together publicity for emceeing two performances. Being onstage, speaking out to a full house filled with both Mexicans and Americans, I felt a level of comfort that reaffirmed my identity not only as a truly bilingual person, but also as a bicultural one. Backstage with the dancers, my American sense of time kicked in as I nervously rushed them through makeup and costume changes between dances. However, as soon as I stepped past the wings, it was as if my Mexican self took over; I spoke calmly and warmly, never once worrying about how many seconds there were left, but simply enjoying the present moment.

BEN CHAMBERS is a member of the Berkeley High class of 2002. He graduated from Claremont McKenna in 2006 and is currently an economic analyst at a San Francisco consulting firm.

My first day on the job, I walked in on pure chaos. The phones at the mayor's office rang incessantly, while reporters paced the hall, peering through the cracks in the blinds hoping to hear a comment from Berkeley Mayor Shirley Dean. Word had gotten out the day before that the city's most powerful landlord was smuggling girls into the United States from India for prostitution and that two of them had recently died. The chief of staff briefed me on the situation, and then directed me to hunt through local newspapers for information relevant to the case. Sitting there with my highlighter in one hand and a pair of scissors in the other, it occurred to me I had been thrown into the thick of a political scandal and was loving every minute of it.

Since this stark first taste of politics, I have interned at Mayor Dean's office for three years and helped the office struggle through two more media outbreaks. Following September 11, Berkeley has been under intense public scrutiny: First the Fire Chief ordered oversize American flags to be taken off fire trucks, and later the City Council passed a resolution denouncing the U.S. military efforts in Afghanistan. Most of the public response and media attention was directed at the mayor's office. My assignment has been to assess thousands of e-mails and hundreds of phone calls from citizens across the country and the world, either berating the city and its "yellow-bellied, pot-smoking, communist leaders" or commending them for their bold statement. My findings help the mayor anticipate the repercussions to the city.

Spending an afternoon each week in such a power hub has been a stimulating experience for me, giving me firsthand knowledge of the difficulties of running a municipal government and the passionate battles between moderate and radical factions that make governing more difficult. I now avidly read the *Berkeley Daily Planet* to follow local political developments.

Working at the mayor's office has intensified my interest in political science, leading me to take as electives Politics and Power, AP Economics, and AP Government at Berkeley High, as well as a Political Science course at Vista Community College last summer. Fascinated by the government policies and the infrastructure that drives societies and economies, I am now strongly considering future studies, internships, and a career in government or economics.

Observing my budding political interest, the mayor's chief of staff suggested I serve on the City of Berkeley Youth Commission. The mayor appointed me to it, and in the two years since then I've learned what it's like to actually be a public official instead of just supporting one. As a commissioner, I've worked on various youth-related projects such as installing a drug-and-alcohol mentoring program in middle schools and setting up a radio station at Berkeley High. I currently lead a subcommittee organizing workshops and forums that educate students about California's recently revised juvenile justice system and what their rights are as minors.

Besides giving me a chance to soak up experiences, my time spent in City Hall has allowed me to realize skills and talents I already have to offer. The mayor's office is run by five middle-aged computer-illiterate women, and just about every week, I put my computer and Internet expertise to work for them. I have taught the staff how to enhance documents using outside images, restructured their system's hard drive to speed up access to files, and reformat important letters and graphics to meet the mayor's exacting standards of visual presentation.

Interning at the mayor's office has provided me an opportunity to serve my community, broaden my horizons for the future, participate in actual politics, and build self-confidence. On top of all this, I have a fun time there and throughout the week look forward to whatever adventure I will take on next. Besides, not many high school students get to discuss with their mayor who the next outcast from *Survivor* will be.

CLAIR LEVY graduated from Berkeley High in 2002. She attended UC Santa Cruz.

Thwack, went the sound of a wooden dildo hitting the side of a desk in order to get the attention of my students. The room filled with shocked gasps, and everyone's eyes cringed.

When I first considered becoming a Berkeley High Peer Health Educator, dread and interest coursed through me. When I was a freshman, I was downright shy. Even around my closest friends I couldn't bring myself to make a decision for fear that I might be criticized. The Peer Health class at Berkeley High was created in order to teach students public speaking skills, as well as have the students talk to their peers about subjects they wouldn't be comfortable talking to an adult about. I signed up, the only freshman in the class, ready to be trained to teach senior guys the proper way of putting on a condom.

On the first day of class, I realized not only was I the only freshman, I would be expected to talk to students about subjects that they might not feel comfortable discussing with an adult. At this point, I didn't feel comfortable discussing some of these topics either. Excitement, dread, and curiosity filled my head. My first few presentations were very difficult, but eventually I was able to make presentations in Social Living classes at Berkeley High, in the city's three public middle schools, and at various private schools. My heart felt like it was going to jump out of my chest every time I had to facilitate a group of seniors discussing the many types of birth control, including demonstrating the proper way of putting on a condom. I grew more in that semester than at any other time in my life. The way I saw myself, as well as the way I perceived others to see me, changed a lot. Now that I'm a senior, I find it amusing to imagine a freshman talking to me about birth control. I also find it amazing that I was able to talk about such mature matters. Talking about sex in front of up to 90 people (some of whom would rather be anywhere but there) just doesn't sound like something I would ever do, which is why it's so surprising to me that I'm still doing it in my senior year.

The class that taught me to be a Peer Health Educator had grant funding that ended after my freshman year. Since then, the program has been an extracurricular activity. As a sophomore, my group's focus was pregnancy prevention. I was again the youngest in the group, but I had come to like that role. I had friends who were juniors and seniors, and when you're a sophomore, it's nice to have friends in high places.

At my school, sophomores are required to take Social Living. So I had to make presentations in front of most of my friends and people I'd been classmates with from preschool on. Can you say "embarrassing"? One of my friends actually made up a song about me after I made a presentation in his class, and would sing it to me when we passed in the halls. Sophomore year was really hard for me. I'm not sure why or how, but I was pretty depressed for about six months that year. I felt that my life was slipping out of my control, but when I was presenting in those classrooms, the control came back and I had some purpose. The only thing I remember looking forward to that year was presenting in Social

Living classes, where I had some control over what was going to happen.

By the end of my sophomore year, I was feeling normal again. Unfortunately, most of the other educators in the program graduated, which left only three experienced presenters with a new advisor. The three of us had to teach our new advisor how to run the program, as well as recruit and train new presenters. I took a leadership role in recruiting people for the program and then teaching them the curriculum. That year, I learned how to be a supervisor and how to solve problems with inexperienced educators.

So I ask again to the class, in what condition does the penis have to be in before putting on a condom? Everyone now yells out, "Hard!" A volunteer stands beside me in the class with a wrapped condom in their hand. I ask them to tell the class each specific step of putting on a condom, saying the step before they actually do it so that if they make a mistake, the student who caught it can make the buzzer noise and tell them what step they forgot. The volunteer can sit down when the condom is on the dildo without any air bubbles between the condom and "pine" and a pinched tip for the semen to go. Before the activity is done, the class must tell me why you would use a condom. The answer is simply, to save your life. And not just to prevent you from getting a deadly disease like HIV, but to prevent pregnancy or a less serious STD that would change your life considerably. Our last activity of the class is to answer any questions that they've written down on index cards. These questions are so powerful, because the students can ask whatever they want without being pinpointed. I help save lives.

COLIN EPSTEIN graduated in 2004. He is currently enrolled at Colorado College, where, among other subjects, he studies dance.

I walked away from the desk, holding my schedule for the upcoming year.

Wait a minute, I thought. *OK, American Lit, Econ, and Government. OK, Latin and AP Bio and Photo. But DANCE?!* There it was on my schedule: Beginning Dance. A class I hadn't requested, didn't want, and had no intention of taking. I resolved to see my counselor and change it as soon as possible.

I filled out a schedule change request form, and waited. And waited. And waited. During all this waiting, I stayed in the dance class. I realized after the first month that the administration wasn't planning to let me switch. I also realized that I didn't really want to anymore. The dance class opened a whole new world for me, a world of movement, rhythm, and expression. It opened a world of wonderful things that I want to be a part of for as long as I can.

I had no idea what to expect going into that class. I had attended the dance shows at Berkeley High School during my freshman and sophomore years, but I had never imagined myself as a dancer. So I was unprepared for what happened in the dance class. To start, there were three guys. And about 30 girls. That was a completely new experience for me, being so much in the minority in a class. Every other class I had been in throughout my school years had been more or less evenly balanced between girls and boys. Then there was the work we did in class, which I had never heard of or imagined. At the beginning, we did a lot of contact improvisation, a very open form of dance that involves weight shifts, balance, and a shifting point of contact between two people. We did things like leaning into or away from our partner, far enough that we were entirely off our center of gravity, finding places to balance on your stomach on a partner, and exploring ways of getting over, around, and through your partner while keeping the point of contact. I think this was a perfect introduction to dance for me, because it was very open, and more athletic, and close to what I had done in the past.

Eight months after that blessed computer error, I find myself backstage, waiting to dance in front of a packed house of about 300 people in Berkeley High's Little Theater. I had dropped a history elective in order to take Dance Projects, a student-run class that ends with an entirely student-choreographed show near the end of the semester. I'm waiting, very nervously, to go onstage for my first dance. I guess I was talking out loud to myself, trying to calm down, and my friend Simon turns to me and whispers, "Dude, chill out. It's just like in rehearsal. Only this time, there's a whole bunch of people watching you."

"Gee, thanks, Simon, that makes me feel so much less nervous."

"Colin, you really need to calm down. Relax. Enjoy yourself. That's why you dance, isn't it?" another friend pipes up.

And I had to admit they were right. The main reason I was standing onstage was because I wanted to have fun. Throughout my life I've played baseball, a little soccer, a little football, done gymnastics, rock climbing, and various other things too, but none of it was anywhere near as compelling to me as dance. Dance is that fun, and it's something that I discovered randomly and loved the experience enough to keep doing it, enough to use my valuable summer time to take more classes and dance more.

To finish the story: Our show was amazing. I realized Simon was right, and being backstage was more nerve-wracking than being onstage. You can't really see the audience, and the rehearsals took over, even through the nervousness that accompanied me onto the stage for my first dance, and before I realized it, I was head-over-heels into a cartwheel at the right moment, and thinking about something entirely different. We danced our hearts out, and the full house loved it, both on Friday and Saturday nights. When the waves of applause washed over the stage, the sheer exhilaration and adrenaline rush I felt was something I had never before experienced. As we wrapped up the show on Saturday, I thought about how far I had come: from someone who was put in a dance class by mistake and wanted desperately to transfer out, to a different person who willingly put on a show for friends, family, and others and danced for fun. It's funny how life works out that way sometimes.

CRISTINE TENNANT, class of 2006, spent a semester of her junior year at the Mountain School of Milton Academy, a farm school in rural Vermont. She is attending Whitman College in the state of Washington.

It was still dark out, and the freezing temperature chilled my California bones. I walked up the winding snow-covered path, the hill just steep enough to get my blood pumping. The sun was starting to rise over the Green Mountains of Vermont, and a sharp breeze pierced my lungs. In my left hand, I carried the yellow basket, and I used my right to pull open the heavy wood door of the chicken coop. When I stepped inside, I was met with both the warmth of the heat lamps and the acrid smell of soiled sawdust and chicken feed. As I approached the hens' nests, a few of the birds looked up at me. One or two ruffled their feathers. Mostly, though, they just ignored me. A particularly scrawny hen followed at my feet, ever hopeful for some extra grain. The air was thick with dusty feathers and gentle clucking. I began to collect the eggs, one by one, counting them aloud as I carefully put them in my basket. Every egg was different—some smaller, some larger. Most were brown, but occasionally one had a violet or green hue. Some of the eggs had just been laid, and I felt their warmth through my thick work gloves. "Sixty-three! Good work, ladies!" I said, to no one in particular. As I carried the now-full basket towards the door, careful not to step on anyone in my path, I prepared myself for the cold outside.

Later, when I was washing the eggs in the harvest kitchen, I thought back to the many times I had eaten, cooked, or even looked at an egg without knowing exactly where it came from. Just three months earlier, I had been working as a short-order cook at Ozzie's, an original 1950s soda fountain in Berkeley, where French toast and egg salad sandwiches were our specialties. Countless times, I cracked open a cold egg onto the sizzling griddle and asked the customer sitting at the counter, "How do you like 'em—over-easy or sunny-side-up?" Never did I contemplate the eggs themselves; I was too busy making sure that no chocolate milkshakes were forgotten and every customer was a happy customer.

A city girl born and raised, I never expected I would learn to love being a farmer. But there I was, using my hard-earned summer bucks to help pay for a semester at a farm school, and feeling more at home in the country than I did in the city. I had been excited about all the challenges of boarding school—leaving my family, living with a roommate, the stimulating academics, a Vermont winter, hard farm labor, and new friendships, but I never imagined that collecting chicken eggs would show me such a deep appreciation for the food I eat.

Today, almost a year later, I realize what a profound influence my time on the farm has had on the direction of my life. I am eager to experience rural life, and to learn how to preserve the environment through sustainable farming. I now have an idea of what I want to do with my life. Eggs were just the beginning.

DANIELLE G. LEVY graduated from Berkeley High in 2005. She is attending Vassar College.

The bright lights of the crowded restaurants illuminate the way as we coast down Shattuck Avenue. I listen and laugh as my friend Jessica presents her latest boyfriend dilemma. We both jump when my cell phone explodes into "Hava Nagila," the Jewish song that is my phone's ring. Grabbing it from my bag, I read "Home" flashing on the screen.

"What now?" I say jokingly, expecting my dad on the line to tell us not to stay out too late, or my mom to tell us to drive carefully because there are a lot of drunk drivers on holiday weekends.

"Dani?" I hear fear in the muffled voice of my younger brother. "Dani, you need to come home right now. Mom needs you."

Six years before my brother's call, on a Friday afternoon in sixth grade, I knew I had had a wonderful childhood. That was also the day my dad cried and cried. It was the day I hated my mom for getting cancer. But after three surgeries and 18 months of chemotherapy, the cancer was gone.

In October of my junior year, exactly five years after my mom's first cancer episode, it came spinning back, messing up everything with the whirlwind of terror, sadness, and lack of control that it brought into our lives. Writing poetry and crying became a daily routine for me.

Now, as I walk quickly through the gate and swing open the front door, I can sense my own fear. I am breathing too hard, and praying for something under my breath—or for *not* something. With my fingers crossed on one hand, I run upstairs to my parents' room. My mom lies paralyzed in pain on the bed, her usually rosy pink cheeks turned white. I should have expected it: It is the second day after the chemotherapy—day two is always the worst.

My dad has gone out for medicine; my brother sits terrified. "Wes, go get her a glass of cold water." I know he needs an escape; 14 is too young to deal with this. I move toward my mom, my breaths quick as if I had just run five miles.

I sit with her for a long time, occasionally rubbing her back or running my fingers through her practically nonexistent hair—"The worst part of chemo," she says. I know that there are worse things, though, when you've been through what she has, but the lack of hair is a reminder of the tragedy.

The hardest part for me has been my powerlessness—the fact that there is nothing I can say or do to keep my mom alive. And although she is a fighter, how much can you fight cancer before it eventually takes control and runs its own course?

My nickname on my rugby team is "Captain Mom," partly because of my leadership as team captain, and partly because I take care of people—by now I am good at it. And in a big way, helping others lets me forget my own pain and allows me to feel good about making a difference in other people's lives. I have found this through coaching a little girls' soccer team for the past two years, and focusing my energy on my girls' needs.

I sit there taking in the soft baldness of her head, the place on her face where her eyebrows should be, the absence of her once beautifully long eyelashes, the ones I inherited. A steady flow of tears trickles down my hot cheeks, but I let them roll because there is nothing I can do to stop them. What I can do, though, is go on with my life and in my own way, try to make the world a better place: Working hard at school and at my job, coaching, playing soccer and rugby, and pursuing social justice give me confidence and show me how strong I am.

DAVID OWEN graduated from Berkeley High in 2002 and from UC Davis in 2006, majoring in communications.

Danny Almonte was the most valuable player of the 2001 Little League World Series, for players of 12 years old or younger. It was later revealed that he was really 14 years old and had been brought by his father to the United States from the Dominican Republic specifically for the purpose of playing in the Series. Almonte and his team from the Bronx were forced to forfeit all wins during the 2001 season.

I am not surprised that Danny Almonte is 14. Shocked? Disappointed? Yes. But not surprised. I spent six springs as a Little Leaguer, and another as a coach, and if I learned anything it was that, too often, honesty and integrity are secondary to success. That is simply the way it is in the world. As I have matured I have seen many examples of this harsh reality, but seldom has it been more painfully obvious than on the sandlots of my youth.

It is hard to say what it was that originally drew me to the game of baseball. I know now, however, what it is that continues to draw me in. When the pitcher faces the batter, nothing else in this world matters. The two men are engaged in a psychological battle as intense as any aspiring gladiator's. They are the only beings on the planet, and time slows down for them. And then, as the pitch is released, the world returns to full speed, with the explosion of bat on ball and the beautifully orchestrated response of the defense. It is poetry. It is beautiful. And I love it.

And yet at times I have hated the game. Mostly I have hated the game from the wooden bench, through the chain links, watching my teammates play the game that I love. That is where I spent too many Saturdays, wanting nothing more than to feel the sting of the ball in my glove and its electricity on impact with the bat. I wanted to be a part of things, but you don't win games by playing the less talented, less competitive kids, and so I sat.

From where did this obsession with winning and "success" stem? My coaches were grown men who apparently needed the recognition associated with winning Little League games. Why were they willing to ruin the experience of kids like me for the sake of success? I wish that I understood how fathers can be capable of casting aside moral obligation in order to win trophies. Perhaps their own self-image is dependent on success at every endeavor. But does success have to be measured in wins and losses?

When I decided to become a coach I hoped to answer that question with a resounding "No," and to give my players the opportunity that I had not had. What I found, however, was that even as a coach it would be impossible to shake the constant presence of the so-called "Little League father," driving his son to win at any cost. I watched as a 13-year-old pitcher bore an abusive workload, and I saw players not unlike myself watching from the bench as I had done, and hating the game as I had done. I wanted to change it, to rewrite this story that had once been my own, but I could not. I could not tell fathers what was good for their sons, so I watched as the young men I had vowed to help were shown the ugly truths that I myself had seen at far too young an age.

In a certain sense I was a failure as a coach. I did not create the environment of support and trust that I had promised myself I would. It was difficult being an assistant, and I do not feel that I contributed to the atmosphere of competitiveness. Still, was I not equally guilty for having witnessed it and said nothing?

It would have been difficult to confront my head coach about the way he ran the team. He was a father, and he was a veteran coach. Still, I had always thought that I cared enough to confront such situations in order to make a positive contribution to my players' lives. Without that effort, how could I ever have expected to create change? Perhaps if not for that same weakness, I might have had a different experience as a boy, and perhaps Danny Almonte would be 12.

Now, as I leave the safety and comfort of high school to enter the next phase of my life, I am sure to encounter less than ideal realities, much as I did as a boy. The most important thing for me, when maneuvering through life, will be to apply the lessons that I have learned in the years since then. If coaching taught me anything, it is that the world truly can be what I make of it. There will be times when it will take a daunting effort for me to make of the world what I believe is right, and I understand now that only by facing this reality can I ever hope to make good in this world. The decisions I make in the next four years will set my direction for the foreseeable future. In choosing that direction, it will be important to maintain a clear concept of success if I am to know what it is that I am pursuing. But what is success? The answer to that question is something that I am just beginning to discover. My coaching experience taught me that success is a very personal thing, defined by something far more significant, and far less tangible, than a trophy. It is an inner sense of fulfillment that comes from confronting fears, setting meaningful goals, and refusing to compromise in the effort to achieve them. If I can pursue success in those terms, I feel confident that the decisions I make will be good ones that will take me where I want to go. Fame and fortune are seductive propositions and provide an easy barometer by which to judge achievement. However, I saw at a young age, and continue to see, the results of surrendering to that temptation. Boys sit, youths are wasted, and Danny Almonte is 14.

DOMINIC CATHEY is currently a student at UC Berkeley. He was able to set the first swim record in Berkeley High's new pool, which opened in April of 2004—just weeks before he graduated.

The summer I turned 12, it was hot. My cousin Jamie and my brother

Lance and I wanted to go to the local swimming pool. We packed up our stuff and started walking, quiet but excited. My cousin remembers that my face lit up with joy every time I heard the words "pool" or "water" come from my little brother's mouth. Like lightning striking from the sky, the sweat falling from my face was worth every moment of going to the pool that day.

We waited in line for 15 minutes, before the lifeguard came out to give the line of children a long reading of the rules and regulations. My mind wandered. Gazing off, I thought how the water would feel against my body. My soul was lifted when I heard the lifeguard say, "OK, that's the end of the rules." The line moved forward and, with my blood sparkling like champagne, I completely forgot about my cousin and little brother. All I could think about was the water. I ran through the locker room toward the pool. I couldn't control all the energy stored inside my body. The lifeguard blew the whistle to start the fun. Everyone jumped into the pool with their teeth shining like pearls, they were so excited.

Leaping off the bottom of the pool, my cousin and I fell into a group of children splashing around, and that's when I saw the deep end of the pool and I knew that was where all the fun was. All I could think about was touching the bottom of 11 feet. I asked one of the lifeguards how I could get over there. My stomach muscles tightened up as I waited for his response.

"You have to take the test; four widths across the pool without stopping and then tread water for one minute." His eyes were still watching the pool as he told me this.

"Can I try?" Intimidated by what was ahead, I started to feel the sweat run down my face, and the sun didn't make it any better.

"Yeah, go ahead." He nodded with an OK, and so did I. I was 12 years old. I had never had a swim lesson. I had never swum in a pool before. The journey began, and acceleration went through my body. It was like rubbing my feet across a carpet before having the electricity run through my body once I'd touched a doorknob. Or the first time ever being sexually intimate with someone. As I finished the test, I looked up at the lifeguard once more with the same smile on my face.

"How was that?" I asked with deep, fast breaths coming from my mouth.

"Yeah, hey, that was great. You ever thought about being on a swim team before?" Now you could finally see his eyes. They were sparkling like sparkling wine that had just been opened.

Since then, I've swum competitively for eight years on the Oakland Under-current swim team and for four years at Berkeley High. I've learned that life's successes often come in small increments. Sometimes even the act of showing up at a workout when your body and psyche are worn out separates a great result from a failure. Swimming has shored up my determination to succeed. But, even more importantly, when I'm swimming a lap up and down the pool in practice, I feel as though it's one of the most peaceful places I've ever been. I can hear the waves crashing against the edge of the pool. There's no one to ask me, "Why aren't you doing this?" or "Why aren't you doing that?" All I can hear is the wind blowing through my hair, and I get the feeling of water flowing around my body.

DORRIE SWANSON graduated from Berkeley High in 2003. She is a student at Tulane University in New Orleans. In the fall of 2005, following Hurricane Katrina, she took classes at three different Bay Area colleges while waiting for Tulane to reopen.

Every Friday I find my thighs sticking to the school's plastic chairs. I spend half of class tugging at my pleated skirt so that it strategically covers as much skin as possible. Friday is Game Day, and, as a cheer-leader, I show my school spirit by wearing my uniform. I have all the makings of an ideal cheerleader: blond hair, a playful attitude, and lots of rhythm. However, at Berkeley High, I am all wrong.

In between classes, my arms are loaded with books as I maneuver my way through the hordes of students to my next class. As a friendly person, I instinctively smile at students I know and even those I do not. I am hit with shouts of, "There goes the white one," as though it is a rare sighting of an endangered species. This is annoying, but I have realized that it is not personal; it is a reflection of the racial climate at Berkeley High. It is a segregated environment behind an integrated facade.

The bell for lunch rattles and the students flock into the courtyard. On "the steps" are the masses of white students meeting each other for lunch. On "the slopes" is the sea of black students doing just the same. Venture into any classroom, and it is clear that Berkeley High students separate themselves. There are traditionally segregated extracurricular activities as well. The white kids populate sports such as crew and la-crosse, whereas black students dominate sports like football and cheer-leading. Despite all the efforts to bring students together, Berkeley High School remains, in actuality, racially divided. As a white cheerleader, I am crossing this not-so-invisible racial line.

I first saw the Berkeley High cheerleaders at Freshman Orientation and was completely in awe of their performance. It was like a finely staged music video, as opposed to the usual cheerleading series of stunts and jumps. The day of cheerleading tryouts, I, a freshman eager to learn the dance routines, was one of 60 girls. I had been dancing since I was able to walk, and as I got older, I found my love for hip-hop. My dance classes were lacking stimulating material, and I thought that cheerleading would provide challenging and innovative choreography. I was anxious to expand my repertoire.

The morning of cheerleading tryouts I was glued to the mirror, the radio blaring, as I repeatedly practiced the routine, swinging my hips to the fast-paced beat. On the way to school I found myself fantasizing a stunning performance with comments like "She was phenomenal" and the reward of a bouquet of spring flowers as victorious music played in the background. What a shock! I was greeted with looks of confusion and anger—I did not belong there; cheerleading was not a "white" thing. By the time the coach posted the roster and I was one of two white girls who had made it onto the varsity squad, I felt as though all the girls hated me. I was invading a space that already seemed small and sacred to them. I felt both discouraged and alienated by the rejection, but I was also unwilling to give up. "Wrong" or not, I was determined to be a cheerleader.

In the course of three days practicing on the rust-colored track, with footballs whizzing over our heads, we learned an eight-minute dance. Next it was time for solo performances in front of all the cheerleaders and the gawking football team. Solo performances? More like a way to prove our worthiness to be squad members, I thought. Dance was the only way I could break the ice and give them a glimpse of who I was. My stomach was in my throat, and my teeth were chattering. I heard the "5, 6, 7, 8" and, having nothing to lose, I let myself go. The energy in the group shifted from hostility to excitement. Samantha yelled, "She's hittin' it!" Shanae screamed, "That girl has rhythm!" Soon, I was no longer performing alone but dancing with the squad as they pulsated and clapped to the beat, shouting in unison, "Go white girl, go white girl . . . "

Over the last four years, we have helped each other learn routines and polish our style. A sense of camaraderie developed because we developed respect for each other and realized we were all there for a common goal: to cheer on the team. I did not go out for cheerleading to defy racial barriers or to learn something about the loneliness of being a minority. I did not stick with it in order to learn about perseverance. Granted, along the way I did learn about those things, but the best part for me is that I made new friends who are vivacious and caring. I am a cheerleader because I love to dance and be with my friends. While the racial climate at Berkeley High is tense, when it comes to cheerleading, being black or white no longer separates us. With only three games left in my last season, I am glad I did not let what has been commonly accepted to influence me in my decisions, my friends, and what I choose to do. My feistiness took me from being the "white girl who can dance" to Dorrie, the friend they call on the weekends to invite to family barbecues.

ELEANOR SMITH graduated from Berkeley High in 2000 and Dartmouth College in 2004. She is currently working for the *Atlantic Monthly* in Washington, D.C., where she still starts her day reading several newspapers.

The *San Francisco Chronicle* and the *New York Times* mean as much to me in the morning as a cup of coffee does to others. It is not my alarm but the pull of the morning newspaper that gets me going. At the breakfast table I drink my juice, fill a bowl with cereal, and arrange the paper so that it is perfectly propped up against two blue candlesticks. Only then do I give myself the pleasure of opening the paper. I have to admit that I start with the entertainment section: the Datebook. I read the comics, several columns, and tidbits such as "Who Said What." I usually have a couple of chuckles as I check out whom Doonesbury is making fun of today and what snippy advice Miss Manners is dishing out. After the humor section, I move to the news. I never get over how much can happen in one day alone. The news can be moving, shocking, frustrating, even thrilling.

What excites me most about the newspaper is how it connects the whole. Every day I read articles not only about my own city and country, but also about the entire world. I love how the newspaper presents new ideas to me and leaves me thinking. When I read the newspaper, I don't forget the articles I read. I think about the issues and read the follow up-articles. I discuss them with my family and friends. I am especially attracted to issues that I've learned about either from my personal reading or from my schoolwork. For example, I recently read the book *Dead Man Walking* by Sister Helen Prejean. It awakened me to the problems in the United States' judicial system and to the death penalty. I read articles related to these issues with growing interest. Recently, I have started to collect newspaper clippings and magazine articles on various topics in which I am interested. I have a stack of articles on everything from the history of World War II to current topics such as gun control.

My love of reading the newspaper did not come out of the blue; when I was little, my parents read to me. I was not such an attentive listener as I am now. While my mom would try to read to my two older sisters, I would jump from my parents' bed into the air, forcing my oldest sister to leap up and catch me over and over again. But as the years went by, books began to lure me. I still remember begging my mom for "Just one more chapter" at bedtime, and when I was older, pausing during homework to hear the story being read aloud to my younger brother.

Joining my school newspaper was a natural for me. The Berkeley High *Jacket* is not a standard school paper. The *Jacket* is an award-winning paper with some 50 students on staff. It comes out every other week and runs from 16 to 20 pages, with a circulation of 3,500. During my sophomore year, I worked on the business staff. That spring I applied to be managing editor, the position that I still hold. As managing editor, I have a vote on the editorial board and am in charge of production, management, and the paper's finances, including raising and managing a budget of $20,000, all of which comes from ads and subscriptions. I learned how to deal with difficult people at the printing press, complaining subscribers, and the school accountant. I transferred bookkeeping to a computer and spent more time at school than most kids would be able to imagine. Being managing editor is, in a sense, the best of two worlds. I am involved in the writing side of the paper as well as the production and management side. I like being in the middle of the action. I am the one people come to when they want to buy a computer hub. I am also the one who says "No" to the insistent staff requests for a refrigerator, microwave, sofa, and even a karaoke machine. However, sometimes I think that maybe my other title should be "Manual Editor." After all, I am the person who carries all the newspapers in from the delivery car, my hands smudged with newsprint. But I'm not complaining. I like newsprint: its cheap smell, gritty feel, and the pleasure it brings me.

ELENA MOSS graduated from Berkeley High in 2005 and is attending the University of Chicago.

In a panel at Northwestern University on what it means to be an artist, the MacArthur Foundation Genius Award–winning playwright and director Mary Zimmerman put forward that artists are those of us who continue to play on into adulthood. She presented an image of dusk on a summer's eve, when children are being called in to wash up for dinner after a long day of imaginative play. Most of the children come when called, but some stay out, and play on into the evening . . . This desire to continue the serious work of play describes not only the temperament of the artist; there is also an aspect of such aspiration that feeds healthy transition into a creative adulthood.

From the time I could reach out and point, I have chosen to study nature guides. My earliest memory is of the rustle of my diaper as I made my way to the sun porch early mornings, to review my books before my parents awakened. I am told that I memorized shelves of laminated six-page animal and plant identification books on whales and snakes and coniferous trees, wowing the local florist when I waddled by his storefront, pointing out the lupines to my mother. But achievement and performance are parental memories; what I remember is the mesmerizing enchantment of Roger Tory Peterson's *Eastern Birds*. This was my primary text, my bible, and my book of fairy tales.

Almost every page of Peterson's guide is illustrated with birds portrayed in identical poses, organized by family and species, and within each species, in different phases of plumage: a male in breeding season, or a juvenile. One species may be exemplified by as many as six images. Each and all of these painted birds are ingrained in my visual memory, so that to this day, when I see a bird for the first time, I recognize it by reference to flat renderings. As a child, I was at first unaware of any correspondence to living beings; even later, what I celebrated was the diversity of the catalogued images as things in themselves. But as I matured, I began to appreciate that the elements of my earliest fantasies were creatures I could bump into in the temporal world! The delight of encountering a living bird that is new to me is a great deal more exciting than the quantification of adding to my life list; it is the adventure of witnessing a fairy tale sprung to life.

There is something of what Mary Zimmerman describes in the uninterrupted continuum of my own fascinations. I have not set my play aside, but have nurtured and developed it, much as an artist grows mature artistic ideas from seeds of childhood imaginings. As my play transforms with the wisdom of growing experience, I am often shocked at the ways in which species I encounter, as a birder, differ from the authority of the tales I absorbed at Peterson's, and later Audubon's knees. I am repeatedly astonished by the size of a bird, astounded by subtleties in coloration that paint and print cannot portray, or taken aback by observable behaviors that are not described in the few brusque phrases of my childhood lore. "Diet: Chiefly fish" cannot express the manner in which an osprey hunts, the way he hurls himself feet first into the water without warning, zigzagging in bent-winged descent so as not to betray himself to his prey by his own shadow . . . It cannot describe the shock of blood on his talons, the way they curve to puncture scaly flesh, a vise grip that cannot be broken. Now I know that even the strongest and largest of fish cannot escape the osprey, or prevail, for not even the osprey himself can break his own grip, and if he misjudges, and sinks his talons into prey that is too large for him to drag from the water, he must bear his mistake to the bottom, still attached to the monstrous fish who could not possibly survive these wounds.

Whereas my colleagues experience birds we watch as curiosities to be identified, I meet new birds as marvelous figments of a familiar inner life become real, and the delight never fails to take my breath away. There is joy in bringing my "play" past its initial stages, enhancing my imaginings with the dimension, detail, and vitality I can add as I gain independence in investigating what intrigues me.

Rather than let go of identifying animal tracks and raising butterflies, get past the passionate study of seashells, edible plants, bats, and snakes, as elements of a tomboy childhood, I have added science reading, an interest in science education, and active membership in a herpetological society to my "play." As a 17-year-old, I devour the likes of Harry W. Greene and David Attenborough for basic animal information. The revolutionary scientific writing of Stephen Jay Gould inspires me; I am stirred by the degree of concentration in Oliver Sacks's observations and the compassion he brings to his science. Within the community, I offer time presenting animals to the young public at the UC Berkeley's science education museum, the Lawrence Hall of Science, and at home I have embarked on a personal project of breeding a rare species of rat snake. I think about becoming an entrepreneur, developing a business in reptile husbandry; I think about becoming a zoo veterinarian; I think about becoming a curator of a zoo collection or at a museum of natural history. I begin to get a sense that while I might have to wash up to get ahead, I will never quite have to come in at dusk, quit the play.

ELI MARIENTHAL graduated from Berkeley High in 2004. He attends Brown University.

Ripe Fruit

Jesse, Dave, and I had camped on the western slope of the ridge the previous night. Shaded by the mountain from first light, we awoke later than normal, not rising until the sun was high enough to reflect brightly off the lake below. Skipping breakfast, we quickly filled our water bottles and headed out toward the southern ridge of Graveyard Peak in the central Sierras. My two closest friends, both of whom were leaving for college the following week, and I have made several important journeys together. This backpacking trip was to be our last for a long time, and the sense of love, companionship, adventure, and imminent loss it entailed had whipped us into a state of continual exuberance. We were just so glad to be with one another that everything was perfect, every occurrence a small miracle. We were in love with life, with the mountains, and with our friendships.

That morning Jesse put into the daypack water, granola bars, his sweatshirt, and a mango. This was an unusual item to have because as any avid backpacker knows, a mango makes a bad traveling companion.

It's heavy, perishable, and messy. We had brought it almost as a joke, dubbing it the celebratory mango. Unsure just what we were going to celebrate, we knew nonetheless that it was an essential ingredient in our journey. For 20 miles we had coddled it, protected it, packed it delicately and carefully, and now it was coming to the summit, up 2,000 feet where the snow never melts and only the bravest birds dare perch. After three hours of scrambling over boulders and crawling through vast patches of gooseberry and young manzanita, stopping occasionally to rest against the trunk of a secure foxtail pine, we reached the summit. The tree line broke to expose the untamable grandeur and immense beauty of the High Sierras. Jesse brought out the mango and handed it to Dave, who gently drew back the skin to reveal an unbroken sphere of golden flesh. When it was split into thirds, the fruit-covered pit saved to be shared later, we delved into our mango. We quickly ate the bulk of our portions, slowing down only to lick the juice from the palms of our hands, using our teeth to pull the small strings of fruit that had been pushed under our nails as we devoured our celebratory mango. As we sat there, sticky and content, I asked rhetorically how anything could be so good. Jesse looked at us contemplatively and said, "I've never allowed a mango to get that ripe before. Usually I eat it as I leave the store. But we've waited four days for this moment, savored the idea of that mango for so long, given it time to ripen, and now we've eaten the best thing that has ever been."

I have devoured these past 17 years, loved them and cherished them. They have left me ecstatic about the possibility of many more. Yet I think I'm going to slow down now, lick life's nectar gently from the palm of my hand, acknowledge the importance of sitting still, cherish the lyricism within the epic of my life and the detail within the bigger picture. I am simply going to allow things to ripen. That which is most precious—love, art, fruit—needs only to be stewarded, given a chance to ripen in the dark unknown of the heart, or of the mind, or even the depths of an old metal-frame backpack.

ELLEN CUSHING, Berkeley High class of 2006, is a student at New York University. This essay discusses the death of Meleia Willis-Starbuck, a Berkeley High graduate. Meleia's college essay is also included in this collection.

My world changed on July 17, 2005, and I changed with it.

As a child of Berkeley, California, the birthplace of the Free Speech Movement and the home of countless demonstrations about everything from veganism to the war in Iraq, I've always considered myself a politically conscious person. I attended my first protest rally when I was still in diapers, and I am passionate about a variety of political and social issues.

To this end, at the beginning of my sophomore year, I chose to enroll in Communication Arts and Sciences (CAS), a program within Berkeley High School that emphasizes social justice. I also joined the staff of our newspaper, the *Jacket,* and these two activities have been the biggest, best, and most important things I've done in high school. In CAS, I have been able to take classes that resonate with me and engage me in valuable discussions, surrounded by perceptive and creative people. On *Jacket,* I have honed my skills and cemented my desire to write for the rest of my life.

These feelings and passions all converged when Meleia Willis-Starbuck, a Berkeley High alumna home on break from college, was shot and killed during the summer before my senior year. Grief and pain spread outward through the concentric circles of my communities: first CAS, which she was also a part of; then Berkeley High School; and then the entire Berkeley community. None of these communities is large, but they feel even smaller when something like this happens.

When the editorial board of the *Jacket* gathered to plan the first issue of the year, the mood was somber. We knew that the story of

Meleia's death and life would be the focus of an issue usually dedicated to anticipatory stories about this year's football team, and I was both honored and intimidated when my fellow editors unanimously chose me to write the article—pleased that I had earned their respect, but worried that encapsulating Meleia's 19-year existence in a thousand words would be like stuffing an elephant into an earring box.

I learned from Meleia's friends and teachers what a leader she was both in and out of the classroom, and I heard stories about her leadership of Berkeley High School's Black Student Union, and her participation in domestic violence prevention efforts. I saw my history teacher, a man I admire immensely, choke back tears as he recalled Meleia's contributions to his class and the CAS community. And suddenly, I found myself mourning someone I had never met, someone I would never meet. It is heartbreaking to get to know and love and be inspired by someone after she is gone.

Meleia's commitment to social justice is what struck me the most. Her example moved me to become more involved with my community, to pay tribute to her not by simply writing an article, but by living a life she would have been proud of. I became a part of the newly formed CAS Race and Equity committee and worked with a small group to plan a six-hour community-building workshop for the senior class. Once school started, I joined the CAS leadership class, and was then selected by my peers to be one of four students on the 12-person CAS Leadership Council. In this group, I can help set the direction for my community by making decisions regarding budget, teacher hiring, and curriculum.

Learning about Meleia inspired me to be a better, more engaged, more active person, to turn this tragedy into something positive. Her days were cut short, so I want to make sure that I use each and every one of mine to effect change.

ELLIE LAMMER graduated from Berkeley High School in 2004 and is currently a student at Tufts University.

The dough is an extension of my hands as I push and spread its pliable mass over the worn countertop. Hip-hop beats pulse, lyrics intertwining with the sweet smells that waft through the house. In the oven, a chocolate soufflé bakes to perfection, the thin crust covering its rich, moist center. The aromas entice my friends to linger, and they bide their time playing cards. The kitchen is a tangle of people. My brother and his friends sneak tastes of the dough, as my parents welcome guests. The crowd impatiently awaits the beep of the timer. My ingredients are sloppily laid out on the counter, nonchalantly scooped into bowls by feel. "One cup flour," reads the recipe, so I throw a handful into a bowl, followed by a pinch of baking powder. The ingredients mix and mingle with my schoolbooks, calculus equations sauté with conversations. My feet are bare and coated in flour, like my trusty red apron.

Years ago, I wore the same oversized apron wrapped awkwardly around my small waist as I stirred a pot while teetering on the edge of a chair. I was fascinated with the mysteries of food, how batter becomes cake in the oven and how to cut an egg in half. My mom shared my passion, and remained calm as I wielded large knives and hovered over boiling pots. Her encouragement and trust inspired me to comb through cookbooks, experiment, and invent my own concoctions. My trademark dish is cake, which I studied in a course where I perfected the art of icing flowers, and in an AP Chemistry project on leavening agents. Sadly, I can't bake a cake every day, so when I come home at six after cross-country practice, a full day of school, and student government meetings, I help my mom cook dinner. The comforting smells of cooking food and the melodic rhythm of chopping vegetables slow the rush of my busy schedule.

Berkeley is a chef's paradise, with fruits, vegetables, and spices from around the world at my fingertips. In January 2001, when I packed my oversized bags for my family's sabbatical in Scotland, I had no idea what culinary challenges lay ahead. We lived in an ancient stone house in a village on the North Sea. The gloomy kitchen contained no more than a tiny box oven and a miniature refrigerator. I joined the crew team at my school and invited the girls over to teach them how to make chocolate chip cookies. The heat of the oven warmed up the dismal kitchen, and the cookies bridged the cultural gap between my new friends and me. Every year, when I go back to visit, I come armed with a supply of chocolate chips.

The mob in my kitchen becomes increasingly impatient, until finally the timer beeps, and I open the oven to reveal a chocolate masterpiece, warm and puffy. My brother pours milk for the throng, some of whom have sat around the table for so many years that they are no longer considered company. I sit down with the steaming soufflé and watch as lifelong relationships blend with budding friendships, and I bask in the beauty of food.

EMMA DONNELLY, a member of the class of 2002, attended UC Santa Cruz.

The sun seeped into my hospital bedroom, its warmth spreading across my swollen eyes. Forcing myself to get up, I slowly moved my legs onto the floor. I gripped the cold steel bed frame and stood up. Dizzy, nauseated, and alone, I walked towards the mirror, dragging a beeping machine behind me. I expected to see my familiar 10-year-old face with wavy brown hair and sunflower eyes, but the reflection I saw in the mirror was that of a stranger. I saw a girl with no hair and bruised skin, her only familiar feature her eyes. I took a deep breath. I was alone with a pitiful survivor. For one long moment I felt immensely sorry for her, for myself. Looking at my reflection, I made a promise never to feel this way again. I did not want to spend the rest of my life in sorrow.

I began having flashbacks of the surgery. I remembered nurses rolling me down white hallways, pushing me into a room filled with bright lights and loud sounds. Strangers in blue masks and plastic gloves held my hands as they sedated me with a gas that smelled like burnt tires and root beer.

When I awoke my Pop was holding my hand. "Do I look different, Pop?" I asked him. "Yes, but you are still Emma." I was told that I had survived a 12-hour craniotomy, and was diagnosed with a rare bone disease called fibrous dysplasia. For the last six years, unknowingly, a tumor had been strangling my optic nerves, causing blindness in my left eye. Although the surgery was a success, and I could already tell an improvement in my vision, I had no way of knowing that two years later my world would grow dim again. Every day it felt like the sunlight was being turned down by an invisible dimmer switch. Dark shadows became my best friends, and I knew that my worst nightmare was coming true. I needed to have another craniotomy.

"Different" is who I have learned to live with. But in the process I felt like I had to conceal this difference from most people because I wanted neither pity nor special treatment. My greatest desire, especially in junior high school, was to be "normal." Hiding my disability was essential because it was my chance to be in a new life. But there wasn't a day that I didn't think about my eyes. I have lived with this disability for nine years and convinced myself that how I see is normal. I have forgotten what it is like to see through both eyes, since I lost my vision in my left eye when I was 10. Nonetheless, with my remaining vision, my world is beautiful.

For a long time I searched desperately to find my passion, my special gift. I will never forget the day I walked barefoot across a smooth wooden dance floor. A woman with chocolate skin and renaissance hair walked into the room. Her presence saturated me with excitement and enthusiasm. Ms. James could leap like fire and twist like the wind. Inspired by this goddess, my dance teacher, I dreamed of being free like her. As days and months passed by, I began to love the sawdust scent of the dance room and crave the coolness of the wooden floor beneath the soles of my feet. Ms. James taught me how to express my whole being through motion instead of words. With this gift she gave me the world.

Before I started dancing I had no place to release my anger, sadness, or joy. Dance freed me of my insecurities and became the voice with which I could express fear and courage, beauty, and grace. Two years later, when I auditioned for Dance Production at Berkeley High School, an intensely competitive and prestigious program, I was accepted. I could only marvel at my transformation from an insecure person to a leading dancer. In a short time I had become a choreographer, lighting director, and costume designer. I had learned how to create unique and beautiful dances of my own.

Dancing fills me up with a wild rush of exhilaration. I am in a place where I am accepted, and no one could guess that this girl flying through the air has a disability. It is my secret, but I can't hide this secret from myself. I am constantly reminded each day of the path that I have traveled, and I am grateful. I do not know if or when I will need to have another craniotomy, but with this unknowing, I choose to cherish what I have now, the people in my life and my future. For myself, I have dance, because when I dance, I am in love.

EMMA SMITH, a graduate in the class of 2005, is a student at Yale University.

I am now a trapeze artist with the potential to realize a professional performing career, one of the few lucky ones who has actually had the opportunity to "run away and join the circus." When people ask me what I do after school and I reply, "I'm in the circus," they usually raise their eyebrows skeptically and conclude that I'm referring to a Ringling Bros.–, Barnum and Bailey–style show, complete with three sawdust-filled rings, parading elephants, and bags of roasted peanuts. However, most circus people now are part of the new wave, Cirque Nouveau, a theatrical spectacle that combines acrobatics, mime, juggling, contortion, trapeze, and other disciplines.

Since I was seven, my instructors, former Chinese acrobats, have told me "Training is bitter," but there are moments in performance that transcend it all. When I hang from the trapeze bar, adrenaline pulsing through my arteries, I forget the searing pain in my palms, the bruises I'm about to earn, the makeup sweating off my face, or how when I get off stage I have to find my juggling clubs for the next act. Right now, it's just the trapeze, the audience, and me. The theater is dark and all the lights are trained on me, glaring into my eyes, nearly blinding me. But I know the audience is out there watching. I can see the red eye of a video camera, the glint of someone's glasses. I feel their eyes fixed on me, and I smile back. I count the music and swing my body under the bar in as wide an arc as I can muscle. I pull up over the trapeze and, resting on my hips, slowly take both hands off, reaching out to that anonymous mass, who I know are waiting, torn between fearing for me at that great height and wanting to be scared. This is, after all, the chills and thrills of the circus. Finally, I fall forward into the trick until I am almost perpendicular to the ground. At the last possible moment, I whip in, riding the momentum of my fall, and spin all the way around the bar. I repeat the trick, gaining speed, listening to the little gasps of the audience. Every time I come around the bar, I look out, teasing them. I am in complete control at this moment. Finally, I throw both arms out to the crowd, hurling myself towards the ground, and at the very last instant, I snake one leg around the ropes, come to an abrupt halt, hanging by one hooked knee, head downwards, my hands blocking the fall I never make. The audience is terrified, but they love it. First afraid and now ecstatically satisfied, they break into applause, cheering for me.

People say, "You can shake the sawdust out of your feet, but you can't shake it out of your heart." And it's true. Circus is deeply ingrained in my life and my heart. For me, there is magic in every performance.

ERIN ANDERSON graduated from Berkeley High in 2007. She plans to attend Yale University.

It's been a long four hours, and I could use a break. The instant I sit down, though, my boss bursts through the swinging door. "We need more plates out there. And get that frittata on a platter. Has anyone started making coffee?" And with a clanging of dishes, she is gone.

Working in the kitchen of my synagogue is no small feat. Putting together an elaborate brunch for a hundred ravenous bar mitzvah guests requires focus and determination, not to mention endless patience. It takes aplomb to smear cream cheese on 200 bagel halves while nervous parents dart in and out of the kitchen, muttering, "Do you think we'll have enough couscous?" and "Where's the coffee?"

When I started working in the kitchen, I was clueless. I leaned in a corner, waiting for my boss to assign me a chore. While scanning the kitchen, I glanced over at the sink. My gaze lingered on the frittata-flecked pans and cream-cheese-smeared knives that spilled over onto the counter, and I knew what I had to do. I marched across the kitchen, rolled up my sleeves, and plunged my arms up to the elbows into the soapy water. My confidence rose with the pile of sparkling plates in the drain rack, and by the time I had emptied the sink, I was ready to take on the world.

Empowered by my success at dishwashing, I attempted more difficult tasks. Slicing pineapple, bussing tables, replacing empty cookie trays: I didn't want to stop for lunch. I worked through break, collecting plate after plate of brownie crumbs and picked-over salmon and loading them into the sink. While before I had shuffled awkwardly around the kitchen, I now strode efficiently, stopping only to pick up empty sugar packets and discarded teaspoons. And whenever I ran out of tables to clear, I marched to the sink, rolled up my sleeves, and started over.

It has been five months since I received my first paycheck, and I am not only comfortable in the kitchen but have learned to apply my catering skills to daily life. I attribute much of my newfound confidence and poise to the time I have spent by the sink. The unpredictable nature of kitchen work has taught me not a specific skill set, but rather a resourceful way of thinking in any situation. Social interactions, formerly my Achilles heel, are now no more intimidating than piles of dirty dishes. Contributing voluntarily to class discussions is easier than clearing tables. I tackle a long and arduous economics test with the composure and persistence I employ when confronted with a mountain of bagels to slice. Prior to entering the kitchen, I thought that opportunities would simply fall into my lap, but now I know that I must seek them. I used to let the dishes pile up, but now I roll up my sleeves and get to work.

ERENDIRA GUTIERREZ, a member of the Berkeley High class of 2000, attended California State University, Chico, and the Dental Hygiene Program at Santa Rosa Junior College.

When the door shut, it slammed so hard I heard the room echo. The room looked so pale and cold, like something you would only see in the movies. Everything was cement and tightly compacted. I sat on the thin layer of cushion that was laid out on the bed for hours, asking myself a hundred questions, repeating myself over and over.

My first idea was to escape. It hadn't kicked in that I had no options. I tried to pick the automatic lock to my door. I even tried to think of a way to melt the nine-inch-thick plastic window to get out. I wondered if anyone even remembered that I was in this room or if I even existed. No sounds. No visitors. Nothing but the deep thump of my heartbeats and the sound of my deep breaths.

The next morning I woke up to the horrible sound of the Juvenile Hall guard's voice telling us to get up and make our beds. I had barely opened my eyes, thinking my bad dream was over. But it wasn't—it had just started.

I was so terrified about what was going to happen. I was in trouble with the law and my family. I was more afraid of coming out than staying in. I was going to be dealing with the toughest family and teachers. I had a lot to think about in 48 hours. I had a weird feeling about worrying my teachers, as they had become a big part of my life. I never thought I would even become close to one. I thought they gave me Fs because they just didn't like me. The truth was that I was at the best high school, where teachers love their students and will take that extra step to make sure that we succeed.

When I was 15, I could have sworn my birth certificate said 21. I even got to live like an adult. But when I was 16, that's where it got bad and my adulthood paid me back. "Erendira Gutierrez, please strip and bend over. Then cough." Those were the words of the woman who left me bare and cold and ashamed. Assault and robbery was what it was called, for my case. The fingerprints, the mug shot, everything I've watched on *Cops* is what I experienced.

At the age of 15, I was known as a juvenile delinquent. Who would have ever thought I would follow in my brother's footsteps? Life was surrounded by gangs, in my eyes. I grew up in a neighborhood where the majority were Latinos who immigrated from all over Latin America. Gangs came in the late 1960s, which carried on from generation to generation. The people I looked up to and the people who I thought I could be with, the ones with the so-called power, were failures, gang members.

The four days I was in Juvie felt like four months. Every time they closed the doors behind me, I felt this bitterness that the system had the key to my life, and in reality it did. Who was I to blame at the age of 15? "The white man put me here," I thought, but the fact was I couldn't blame anyone but myself. It was the Chicana girl that put herself here.

The two people that I was mostly worried about were my aunt, Beatriz, and my teacher, Mr. Ayers. They both had done a lot for me to achieve. I was embarrassed and ashamed. They both had tried to keep me out of trouble, but there was nothing they could say or do to change my mind. I had to find it in my eyes. Two thoughts, giving in to my gang or proving myself for the rest of my life. It had to be one or the other that was more important to me.

When I was a little girl, I always wanted to be like my Tia Beatriz, who I thought was mean and smart, a very strong Chicana with a perfect family that included a dog. I could only think she was very lucky, but now I was starting to realize that it had nothing to do with luck. At this point, I had to think about what was best for me—having everything she had or not knowing if I'm going to live the next day or not. I had to think if my gang was going to make me happy or if I should go to college, get a good job, education, and have a family of my own.

All these points laid out for me made me change so quickly. My outlook, my views, my friends, my attitude changed. Here I am today, May 1999, at UC Santa Cruz, getting some help from college students. They are helping me to write this college admission essay. Sitting with one of my classmates whom I hated during my sophomore year because I thought she was too smart, telling her my story and asking for her opinions.

I never once thought that I would make it this far or even visit a college to write an essay for my future. I'm thinking right now, and looking back, even if it was a few months ago, how stupid and selfish I was. I was making myself think I was going to become someone bigger with power. The real power is what good things you do with your life. I know that college is just the beginning of those good things for me.

GEOFFREY SHAMES, a member of the Berkeley High class of 2005, is currently a student at Boston University. He writes about his dear friend Nic Rotolo, also a member of the Berkeley High class of 2005, who died in the middle of their junior year.

A Heart Torn Apart

It was going to be an adventure for the ages. As we were a group of four 17-year-old boys, our planning for the trip was almost nonexistent. On the last day of school, the boys and I were going to jump into our cars, go to the airport, and spend the whole summer in Europe. We were going to fly into England and stay there for a few days, then buy Eurail passes and explore all of Europe for the rest of the summer. That was the extent of our plans. The whole idea was for Nic, Slither, Sam, and me to explore the other side of the world—no plans, no parents, no end to the fun.

We were always planning things like trips to Europe. We had plans to start our own clothing company, plans on how we were going to be successful, even plans on where we were all going to be in 50 years. We always did everything together, and we were all as close as brothers and planned to stay that way for as long as possible. That was all taken from us one night with one quick, static-filled cell phone call.

Around 9 p.m. on February 5, 2004, I picked up my phone to hear a single sentence that would change the rest of my life. As soon as I picked up the phone, there was a strange silence that made my heart skip a beat, and I knew this wasn't a social call. The next three words that came out of my friend's mouth are still echoing in my head as I write this. It's really amazing how three simple words can send your whole life into a downward spiral, even before you have a chance to really think about what is being said. When I picked up the phone all I heard was "Nic is dead."

Upon hearing those words, my heart instantly seized up and I lost control of the muscles in my legs, landing on the floor in complete shock and bewilderment. At first I denied the whole thing. The idea that a 17-year-old boy in the best shape of his life, using no drugs or alcohol, and with no history of heart problems, could collapse dead in an instant just made no sense to me. After a few minutes of disbelief, emotions coursed into my mind like a tidal wave. The best part of my life had just been stripped from me. By some twist of fate, my best friend had just died of a sudden massive heart attack while playing ice hockey, something he did all the time. My emotions went from anger and wanting somebody to blame, to absolute depression and not knowing what to do with myself. That night, all of us who had been close to Nic cried in one big mass of sorrow, and quite honestly it brought us closer together than we ever had been before. Now we are more like a very close family than just a group of friends.

On the first Sunday of every month, we all meet at Nic's old house and have a dinner party in his memory. Every time, there will be a few people who are feeling depressed, and there are always people there to comfort them. I'm writing this essay right now having just returned from one of these Sunday-night dinners at Nic's house. This dinner was especially significant because it happened to be on Nic's birthday, which would have been his 18th. We all went to his house and went through our normal routine of eating great food, telling jokes and old stories about Nic, and just generally being there for each other, but this time we also did something more. Since it was Nic's birthday, we all brought candles and went out to the backyard and sang "Happy Birthday" to him. It was the most amazing spectacle of people getting together and helping each other out that I have ever witnessed.

While losing Nic was the worst tragedy I have ever faced, I also learned a great deal about myself and people in general because of it. I have learned that it is important to live life to the fullest in every second you have, and to try to achieve as much as you possibly can in the time you have in your life. You never know when everything may be taken away from you, so you have to take action when the opportunity arises. I have learned that there is always somebody out there who genuinely cares about you and wants you to succeed in life, and that you can always count on them to be there for you through good times and bad. It is truly a beautiful thing.

GRACE GILL graduated from Berkeley High in 2005 and is attending the University of Southern California.

Oi!!! Come here, girl. You said you wanted curry, you're 17, now get yourself over here and help me make it!!! When I was your age, my mama shouted, I made an entire buffet consisting of seven different main courses and 100 rotis and gulaab jamans. You're going to college now, what are you going to eat there? I won't be there with you, you know!! Come here now, Grace Gill!

Considering that I don't have a middle or a long first/last name, the effect isn't that impressive. Perhaps . . . *Come here, Jaswinder Patti Gill!* Note the difference. OK, OK. Trudging my feet like a pack mule being sent to the slaughter, I enter the steamy kitchen. Immediately, my eyes start to water. The spices assault me. I am yanked by the arm, and a plate of onions, garlic, ginger, parsley, and green pepper is shoved under my nose. *Cut. But Ma. . . . CUT!* My beautiful, serene mother suddenly looks like a really angry Emeril Lagasse, the frenzied TV cook. Not that I mind cooking, I love to cook, but curry is like a woman, very fickle and high maintenance. Actually, it's like me. Curry is the culinary representation of moi.

I stare dumbfounded at the spices and slowly begin picking them up and awkwardly cutting them. Slice, slice, slice, sugar and spice make every dish nice. Oh, hush up, Gill. Now is not the time to practice your rhyming skills. I had been practicing on my tabla, my beautiful Indian drum set, before I was kidnapped by my mother. Well, maybe I'll cook the curry to the rhythm of the tabla. Cut, cut, cut, slice and dice. *DhaDha Dhina Tin, Na Tin Na Tin.* Eyes screwed against the sting, I slice the ginger. The juice spurts out and smacks me in my eye. OWW! I hop to the rhythm of the drums in my Afro-Haitian dance class. Boom, boom-boom. In the living room my father sits with his whiskey, watching TV. He laughs, and his great big belly shakes like a bowl full of jelly. He grins at me. He knows he can sit there in his glorious personage while the womenfolk cook. *Oh, you useless girl.* My arm is pulled again, and I find myself face to face with the bubbling curry, with my eye twitching ferociously. I don't know what to say. It looks really yellow and hot and angry. Stir the curry. I take the ladle and stir, trying to soothe the savage beast.

My mom's Lata Mangeshkar is drowned out with Kanye West's new rap song, "Jesus," on the radio. "Jesus walks with me, with me." I hum to the lyrics.

No, not Jesus. You're not Christian. Guru Nanak walks with me, with me.

I look at the curry. Now it's bearing a resemblance to the substance

I eat. Feeling a little bouncy, I stir some more. Now I'm feeling rather . . . intrepid. The aroma of the spices mingle flavorfully in the curry, and the color takes on a golden hue. It thickens and bubbles softly. Absurdly pleased, I grin and catch the confused eye of my mother, who is staring at me. *I was thinking of this joke someone told me,* I stammer. Her raised eyebrows leave no doubt that she doesn't believe me. It's OK. Mama's always known I'm weird and a persistent daydreamer. The green leaves in the curry swirl about and add dimension and flair to the dish. My arms flex, and I move them rapidly, like the blades of the mixer, which are currently pulverizing more ginger.

At last, the curry has been tamed like poor Kate, though I don't think Shakespeare had curry on his mind when he wrote *The Taming of the Shrew.* Ah well, back to my drums. Now I can re-enter my haven. *Where you going?* My mother's softly inquired question makes the fine hairs on my neck stand. Sounds suddenly seem distant, like one of those dramatic scenes you see in the movies. *Girl, you haven't even started on the rotis yet!*

HANNAH SARVASY graduated from Berkeley High in 1999 and Harvard University in 2003. She is a former Fulbright Scholar in the Netherlands, and her graphic novella *Dear Brother* debuted at the 2006 Haarlem Stripdagen comics festival.

"Graciousness," my mother spit, wild-eyed, "graciousness!" She whirled and banged the pot onto a burner. I flinched at the clang of metal crashing against metal, but slunk back to my cello in the living room to investigate a particularly hard passage of the Haydn Concerto in D. It wasn't my fault my name meant "graciousness." My mother had named me

Hannah after her grandmother, and if that wasn't the best name for me, well, whose fault was that? She certainly could not shame me into apologizing for our argument by reminding me of the meaning of my name.

I was always glad that I had not inherited my surname as well from my mother's side of the family. Her last name was Sondik, a name that in old times was used to refer to the man who held the baby during the Jewish circumcision rites: not exactly the most glamorous of titles. From my mother's family, however, I did inherit rough-hewn stories of the Jewish Old World.

My mother's aunt told us that a drunken *muzhik* (Russian soldier) shot and killed her grandfather, leaving his 11 children orphans. Her father, Zavel, was the youngest, at two years old. It so happened, my great-aunt said, that Zavel and his brothers and sisters did pretty well as they grew older (considering that they were orphaned, destitute, and Jews living in Russia: thrice cursed!). One of Zavel's brothers suffered a severe setback, however, while attempting to escape the compulsory Russian military service. He went to a peasant charlatan for help, who gave him a powder to rub in his eyes. She told him it would blind him temporarily for the duration of the army examination, but the ensuing blindness proved to be permanent, and he was barred from both Russian military service and, years later, immigration to the United States. He had two children in the Ukraine, Gitel and Izik. As with most of my relatives who did not emigrate, I assume that they perished in Hitler's crematoria.

Old stories like this one always intrigued me, as did old objects and people. In the summer I wandered sometimes through the downtown Berkeley streets purged of college students. Even as I reveled in the bright morning sidewalks glistening with dew, junk-store windows caught my eye. Dusty chests, frosted-glass medicine bottles, and boxes of old photographs placed strategically near the door of an antique store invariably sucked me in, helpless, from the sidewalk; I would stumble out into the daylight hours later, dazed, 75 cents poorer, having perused the store's entire collection of miscellaneous photos circa 1925.

I first volunteered in a nursing home when I was 10 years old, in sixth grade. I adored the residents of the home: the wizened men bowed over the plastic trays of their wheelchairs, the three keen-eyed, murmuring matrons from whom I learned the nursing home lore, and the old blind woman who took my hand and, sighing, pressed it to her cold wrinkled cheeks.

Recently, I volunteered in a local Home for Jewish Parents with a blond, blue-eyed friend named Jeffie. We approached a resident together, Jeffie introducing herself first. The old woman asked Jeffie to repeat her name several times; she seemed to have trouble understanding her. But when I began, "I'm Hannah," the old woman's laugh dwarfed her shrunken body. "Now *that's* a good Jewish name," she said, gazing at me.

And so it is. . . . Jewish tradition maintains that the chain of life remains unbroken when babies are named after dead relatives. The relatives live on in the growing children who share their names. When those children reach adulthood and die, they pass on the names of their predecessors to a new generation. Every time I sign my name, my great-grandmother and the long line of women whose name *she* bore are memorialized in print. The name does not only belong to me, but to the long line of Jewish Hannahs that reaches back to the bereaved barren woman of the Torah whose woeful entreaties caused God himself to weep.

Perhaps it is because so many limbs of my family tree were severed in the European bloodbaths of the 1930s and '40s that I have adopted for myself a relatively strict code of honor. Whether I like it or not, nothing I do is for me alone, but for all of my antecedents who were named Hannah. I cannot allow myself to desecrate my name through dishonesty, cruelty, or any other means, because in so doing I debase my people.

I laid my cello down carefully on the soft low piling of the living room rug. Turning in the direction of the kitchen, I inhaled deeply, summoning the strength of my great-grandmother and her ancestors. "Mom," I said, "I'm sorry." As I exhaled, I felt the anger ebb from my body and the warm sensation of relief flood my face. I had done the right thing, I was sure of it, and I knew Hannah and Hannah, and Hannah, would have approved.

HENRY CORRIGAN-GIBBS, a member of the Berkeley High class of 2006, is attending Yale.

It was complete and utter chaos. A sea of students stood shoulder to shoulder in a large courtyard, organized into one huge, snaking line. Teachers, many of whom looked like students themselves, scurried around frantically. It was orientation day at Berkeley High, and 1,000 students were waiting to get their photos taken. There was only one camera.

I was one of the young freshmen waiting in the August heat that day, and it was my first experience with Berkeley High. I arrived 20 minutes early (to beat the crowds), brought $5 (for lunch), and figured it would take a half hour (tops). But by the time I stepped on campus that morning, it seemed that I was the last to arrive. It became immediately clear that I certainly wasn't going to use my lunch money, seeing as I would still be at school through lunch. And, as I would soon discover, when 1,000 students are involved, nothing takes a half hour.

As the morning dragged on, the students grew restless. Water balloons sailed across the courtyard, and what began as a line devolved into an undulating mass of increasingly impatient teens. Hoping to quell the brewing riot (or not knowing what else to do), the administrators herded the entire crowd into the school's cavernous theater.

Inside in the theater, the hum of post-summer conversation soon filled the stale air. Impromptu games of cards were set up in the aisles, with teachers and students camped out next to each other. All around, students introduced themselves to the people sitting close by, hoping to make a new friend and pass the time. As the lunch hour rolled by, some enterprising students made pilgrimages to the 7-Eleven, with snack orders for their friends. Eventually, a small woman appeared on the stage with a megaphone and began directing students to leave the theater and get their pictures taken. I was one of the last to be called, and left the school with my ID card just as the sun dipped below the horizon.

In the three long years since my freshman orientation, I am discovering more and more how the skills I have learned at Berkeley High have not only aided in my success at school, but also in life in general. When traveling in Cuba, my extensive experience dealing with the school administration proved helpful in dealing with the ubiquitous Cuban bureaucracy. The self-reliance the school gave me was invaluable during my summer job at a software company. (Lacking formal training, I ended up teaching myself how to do most of the job at my desk out in a storage warehouse.)

But beyond these material skills, Berkeley High has given me the benefits of an institution where the most interesting events happen by chance. Lectures about communism in government class end up with Russian immigrant students discussing the virtues of the American democratic system. The final projects of one media class evolve into a public film festival covering every topic from the death penalty to the life of the school custodian. And the freshman photo day turns into a social event for the student body. By keeping an open mind to the constant surprises offered by a large urban high school such as mine, I've been able to get more out of my time at school than I ever could have imagined.

This week, I go back to Berkeley High for my last orientation. I'm curious to find out what this year will hold.

IAN ROSE graduated from Berkeley High in 2005 and is currently a student at Yale.

Life is complicated; an ongoing juggling act of tasks to complete, friends to keep, sports to play, and the need to keep up in my classes. Regardless of how much I do, there is always something more hanging overhead. Every once in awhile, life's demands seem to grow far larger than is reasonable, with no solution or end in sight. That is when I go for a walk.

I live in Berkeley, directly across the bay from San Francisco. When I walk, I step outside of my home with no particular destination in mind, and if I begin early enough, no time limit. Soon I refine my direction to things like "up," or "north," or "I wonder if I can find my way to the top of that hill in the distance?" Often my wanderings lead me to Tilden, a regional park in the hills to the east. From the hillside there is a commanding view of San Francisco and much of the Bay Area. Other times I end up at the waterfront, watching people sail boats and fly kites. Sometimes I bring a book, but my destinations tend to be too windy to make much progress, so it ends up being just for show.

I enjoy these walks because they allow my mind to wander free and unfettered. So much of my time is spent doing what I need to do as a student, a teen, or a son; these things follow me around sneakily even during my leisure time. When I walk, I bring no homework, no cell phone, and no study material. If I've chosen my destination well, it is unlikely that I will encounter anyone I know, and I will be at least a few hours away from the tasks that await me. I will have no excuse but to think about whatever I want. It is impossible to do otherwise.

Inevitably I spend much of my time staring into the distance. I love to watch the beauty of the San Francisco skyline, the colossal cranes at the port of Oakland, and civilization as far as I can see. I love the size and shape of the skyscrapers in the distance. And I love then noting that the smallest hills dwarf the largest buildings in sight. Above all, I love the enormity of the world, and the feel for the region around my home that only a person on foot can know.

When I return home several hours later, I am often tired, but my mind is well rested and ready to re-enter the world. I still have essays to write, homework to do, practice to attend, appointments to keep, and one less day for them all. But despite this, I consider my walks to be time well spent.

JACK NICOLAUS graduated from Berkeley High in 2005 and is currently a student at UCLA.

My letter jacket often clashes with my leotard. I find myself quoting Shakespeare in the middle of wind sprints. When I flub a line, I have an urge to do pushups in order to punish myself. I live in two worlds. In the theater community I'm viewed as an enigma. Why would a smart, sensitive, talented actor partake in the macho, violent world of football? On the football field I'm seen as a puzzle. After all, why would a football player waste his time being introspective and artistic? I find that inside my own head these two images of myself clash, then begin to meld together, and finally combine to form the antithesis of all stereotypes. I'm a macho actor and a sensitive jock. I share my time between stage lights and stadium lights.

I have found my niche in these two different social scenes, but I see the similarities every day of my life. Juggling the pressures of being the only football-playing actor can sometimes get to me. During football season, it's hard to find time onstage. When the season is over, it's hard to keep me off it. For the past three years immediately following the season, I've helped produce and act in a completely student-run theater production, without any help from adults at my high school. Rehearsals start almost immediately, but athletes must tend to their bodies, and I manage to find time for the "voluntary" (football-coach-speak for "Legally I can't require you to come") workouts four days a week. One day sticks out in my mind particularly. I was performing the role of Bug Jule in *Guys and Dolls* for Berkeley High's musical. It just so happened that the musical was running concurrently with the football team's spring mini-camp. My coach was gracious enough to excuse me from practice when rehearsals conflicted, but on performance nights I didn't have to be at the theater until 6 p.m. He and I saw no reason why I couldn't go to practice until 5:45 or so and then run over to the other side of campus to the theater and get ready to act.

Practice started promptly at 3:45. I am team captain, so I led the stretches. We started our calisthenics and worked up a good sweat. During the water break I shuffled absentmindedly through my choreography. The guys around me chuckled at my awkward movements, but I paid them no mind. Practice continued. I became swept up in the macho posturing and yelling so frequently found on a football field. By the time the clock struck 5:45, I was drenched in sweat and my adrenaline was pumping. I ran off the field and changed into my regular clothes, but since there was no time for a shower, I arrived at the theater smelling of sweat and Old Spice. I donned my costume and had my makeup applied. My muscles were beginning to stiffen up. I stretched the only way I knew how. As my castmates did the stretches they had learned in dance class, I did my football warmup. My castmates chuckled at my awkward movements, but I paid them no mind. As the show approached, I helped lead the cast in a group warm-up. We could hear the theater filling up.

The curtain rose and the show began. With every scene break and wave of applause from the audience, I felt my excitement surge. When the show-stopping number hit its last note, the audience exploded. I was drenched with sweat, and my adrenaline was pumping.

JASON KATZ-BROWN, class of 2004, is now study-ing at the Massachusetts Institute of Technology.

MASSACHUSETTS INSTITUTE OF TECHNOLOGY PROMPT
Life brings many disappointments as well as satisfactions. Could you tell us about a time in your life when you experienced disappointment, or faced difficult or trying circumstances? How did you react?

My greatest disappointments and satisfactions have come from my campaign to make Linux universal. I started using Linux, an alternative free-software operating system, four years ago as my full-time operating system and fell in love with it. As I found my passion for computer science, I joined with the worldwide group of open-source software engineers to work on making Linux easy to install and use. I decided to combine my passions for computer science and the Japanese language, which I had been studying for several years in school, to encourage Japanese users to switch to Linux.

Making the programs available on Linux easier for Japanese to use was my first step. I wrote a Japanese dictionary and study tool, named Kiten, which is now shipped with all Linux distributions, which is the operating system plus selected applications that are freely available. I was excited about my contributions and on a roll.

In July 2003, I was invited by Softopia Japan, a high-tech center near Kyoto, to deliver a presentation in Japanese about open-source software development. My goal was to show businessmen how to leverage open-source development for cheaper, more reliable software. The group of about thirty high-tech executives understood what I was saying and showed interest, but I felt like proprietary software was so firmly wedged into their businesses that it would take much more than a talk from me to convince them to use Linux. They were polite, but distant from my talk; it seemed as if nothing changed despite my best intentions and weeks of hard work.

This experience was intensely disappointing. I could see that the execs saw the future in Linux, but were daunted by the prospect of the switch from Microsoft. No matter what I had said, I did not have much power to effect change. When I thought about what was stopping them, I realized I also needed more engineering skills to design open-source solutions that would appeal to big business in Japan.

However, another opportunity arose around the same time. I figured one more way I could help Japanese Linux users was to write an improved Japanese input method for graphical Linux interfaces. I disliked not knowing what was going on when somebody types in text that magically turns into the correct Japanese characters. I wanted to understand the magic and make it work better. This was a much harder engineering task than I had faced previously, and frustration was a constant companion in the months of programming before my program actually did anything at all. But I used a modular architecture so I could skip around during development, and I enlisted the help of many online friends when I did get stuck.

Most importantly, I have made Linux easier to use, and while I haven't reached my goal of making Linux the Japanese operating system, I have made a good start. I learned a lot from this experience about how to deal with disappointment. Now I try to find stepping stones en route to my goals. I also learned to push on when things don't turn out as I hoped.

JENNIFER BURKS graduated in 2004 and is currently a student at California State University, East Bay.

My grandma was abruptly awakened at 3 a.m. on a foggy Saturday morning. She was informed that her granddaughter was in an overnight foster home located in Sacramento, California. She was there because her mother was caught in a stolen vehicle while driving 110 miles per hour. She rushed to the scene as quickly as possible. At that moment, I felt the system start to take over me. I went to my first foster home and went to many after that.

Being in foster care was really terrible. However, my grandmother always made it not so bad. She always kept me active and feeling like I was just as smart and just as talented as the other children were. My grandma was my foster parent for 11 years before she passed away from lung cancer. She always encouraged me to start and complete as many goals as possible. With that strong motivation and drive, I began to look for certain activities that seemed interesting to me.

I took one step toward my goals when I joined Teens Teaching Tobacco Prevention. I started this my freshman year at Berkeley High School, because I saw too many of my friends and family beginning to smoke, and I wanted to teach the younger children that it wasn't cool to smoke.

Echoing my passion for working with children, I began to work with the youth and children of my church. We put on programs such as musicals, pageants, and Vacation Bible school. We also went on field trips and attended important events, including hearing motivational speakers talk about how to improve a church community. My second goal was to teach foster children that life isn't as bad as the media and society portrays it to be. I wanted them to understand that there is a whole world out there for them to learn and explore.

I have really tried to help as many foster children as I can because I don't know how much longer I will be on this earth, and I want everyone to know who I am. A motivational speaker once told me: "It isn't how many years you have in your life, but how much life you have in your years." Ever since I heard that saying, I have learned how to cherish every moment as if it was my last. I do now understand that I won't touch everyone, but I can reach as many foster children and youth as possible.

Despite my impediments, I have triumphed and achieved more than society ever expected of me. I am proud to be a part of the Beating the Odds Club. I know that I am a lifetime member, and unfortunately too many children who shouldn't have to join are joining. I know that I want to go to college, however, I'm not yet sure what I want to do after college—but I know that I want to work with foster children. I have an everlasting dream to prevent as many foster children and youth from having to go in the system. That is why I have such strong determination to make a change in the world. It is up to us to make a difference in the world, because no one will do it for us.

JERMELLE NEWMAN **graduated from Berkeley High in 2004 and is a student at the University of San Francisco.**

The most soft-hearted voice one could ever hear was my mother telling me to keep hope alive and never give up. That statement has always stuck with me and gives me confidence to succeed. I have succeeded in school. I will be the first member of my family to go to college. I am very proud about that, and I gain pride in making my family happy with my success.

I love to learn and I have pushed myself to take advanced classes that will prepare me for college. This year I am taking three Advanced

Placement courses and one Honors course. I am one of the few African American students in those classes—for example, AP Lit. has only three black students. When I first walked through the door all I saw were white people, staring at me, probably wondering how I got into that class. I still feel like I'm in a "different world" in my classes. I feel like a visitor in a foreign land. I took the initiative to find out about the place. First, I had to go through customs (school counselor) to get permission to go there. Then I had to get a passport (report card) in order to get where I wanted to go. I had to speak and act a certain way, to "obey the customs." With my black peers I speak slang because that's the way we communicate. I act more comfortably around them, because we understand each other. I have learned to communicate with the students in this new land, by expanding my vocabulary and conversation skills, by learning a new dialect.

Berkeley High School is a large urban school with incredible diversity and a wide variety of academic offerings. If one walks on campus one will see segregation between races—students tend to associate with people of the same race. You will see me having conversations with all different kinds of people, because I believe in maximizing the opportunity to connect with people and learn from all different types of people. Now I have learned to be fluent. I learned about different cultures and how to interact in a multicultural world. Also at Berkeley High there's a huge achievement gap, between white students and black and Latino students. This is an enduring problem that has dampened the Berkeley community. My presence in advanced level classes goes against the school's culture. Mostly white students take Advanced Placement courses. In the reality of Berkeley High it's not normal for me to be in Advanced Placement courses. None of my friends that are black are in the same classes as me, and it's heartbreaking to me to notice that. And I know that there are a lot of African American students that can be in the same land, if they apply themselves like I did.

Being in a class surrounded by white students is an advantage for me because I learn about their culture and how they operate. What I learn in the classrooms, combined with my cultural background, gives me an edge. I have the best of both worlds. I am like a bridge that links two different lands together, closing the achievement gap.

Joanna Jacobs graduated from Berkeley High in 2005 and is currently a student at Brown University.

What if I'd had a "normal" sister? This is a question I constantly ask myself. My older sister was diagnosed with a brain cancer when she was 15 months old. I don't remember this because I wasn't even a fleck of an idea in my parents' minds. The doctors treated her, they did the surgery, the radiation, the chemotherapy, everything. And, in time, the tumor was gone. All that was left was a young girl with a big scar on the top of her head, the beginnings of an epilepsy disorder, and some mental disabilities. She was barely two years old, and she'd already surpassed her life expectancy.

As she grew older, and I came into the picture, her mental handicaps and her epilepsy continued to get worse. The reasons for this, I was told, were because the doctors at that time hadn't completely understood the side effects of too much radiation to the brain.

But that's all water under the bridge now, because my sister is simply the person she is. She is definitely developmentally disabled. She is definitely epileptic.

I've always been haunted by questions, wondering how my life would have been different if those cells in my sister's brain hadn't started multiplying out of control. What kind of person would I be today? The only answer I can think of is: a very different one.

Growing up around a mentally retarded person means practicing patience, all the time. I've learned to hold myself in check while waiting for my sister to form coherent sentences. I've sat holding my tongue as she takes half an hour to make a sandwich with tuna fish from a can. It is a few simple things like that that I've learned.

But what have I lost? This is the unanswerable question. I guess you can't miss what you never had, but it certainly is difficult when you have friends with older sisters. You see them receiving the hand-me-downs, having the fights, and getting the advice about boys. You see them make mistakes and learn from them. These are things I'm worried to have lost, and I blame those silly multiplying cells. It's difficult to think about.

However, I try not to dwell on the "what ifs" too much because they hurt, and I feel alone. I've been lucky, though—my sister is a truly wonderful and giving person. I'm not sure if she realizes all the things she's missing in life, not to mention the things I feel I'm missing. Because of that, though, she's happy. For her, ignorance must be bliss. But for me ignorance is no option. I live with the fact that some disease and the way it was treated robbed me of the "normal" older sister that should have been mine.

I'm not the same person I might have been, but inevitably I am myself, created by my environment, the good and the bad. Ultimately, I believe, my sister has made me a better person.

JOSEPH SHEMUEL graduated from Berkeley High in 2007. He planned to attend Columbia University.

I was blessed with neither good handwriting nor the ability to do much of anything dexterous, at least without the aid of a keyboard and mouse.

As a child, my penmanship was more quickly identified as Sanskrit or gibberish than English, and my hand-drawn artistic abilities stopped just shy of the well-proportioned stick figure. My parents had been computer users since the Kaypro, so as soon as I could sit on a lap and hold the mouse, a computer was the natural choice for me.

The computer, however, wasn't initially a tool, but a way for my parents to subliminally educate me. To help me understand letters, they plugged me into games like Reader Rabbit. (Kids love alliteration, evidently.) I partially attribute my love of reading and writing to sounding out consonant blends as his bushy tail hopped from letter to letter. Reader Rabbit and I got along well at first, but I eventually decided that I had read enough inane stories about Cathy Cow and Danny Duck. It was time to start writing my own barnyard epics.

Since I first typed out "Jonah the Happy Moose" in third grade, I haven't stopped writing. It has become a passion for me, almost an addiction. I write when I feel aggravated, relieved, overwhelmed, or just generally open, churning out several pieces a month, most of which never leave the screen. Recently, it all paid off as I won my first writing contest and publication in a local newspaper. But none of it could happen without my computer, because over the years, my declining penmanship has made me averse to writing by hand. By granting me the simple privilege to type, my computer has been integral to my writing.

In this way, my experience with the computer has undergone a role reversal: Instead of commanding me via the words and gestures of childhood cartoons, the computer now does as I dictate with the mouse and keyboard. Instead of a crutch, it has become an invaluable resource. On a basic level, I use it to do mundane work such as word processing and spreadsheets. Since I still can't draw anything recognizable with my hands, I've learned to use programs like Adobe Photoshop, which allow graphic professionals and amateurs alike to create almost any kind of two-dimensional graphic. I've designed everything from flyers for

Frisbee-team tryouts, to graphics for the school newspaper, to a logo for a local DJ crew, The Rock-It Scientists. My art, and thus, my computer, have been as much for my friends and clients as for my own fulfillment.

But of course, my computer is not only educational and creative. It's first and foremost, as the folks at Facebook would like you to believe, intensely social. Similarly, the reputation of the computer as the anti-social geek's lovechild has disappeared; instead of insulating the user, the computer almost mandates contact with our friends, providing several different, yet simultaneous, ways to interact. For some people, the method of choice is e-mail or instant messenger. For me, it's the blog, which allows me to share my political commentary and personal inclinations with hundreds of interested readers worldwide. I could go on for pages just about the Internet and the way it has revolutionized our lives.

This December, *TIME* magazine chose its Person of the Year to be the ubiquitous "You." The cover featured only a computer, complete with a reflective panel for the monitor. When I picked it up off the newsstand a week ago, I saw myself staring back. This is how I often think of my computer; over the years, the monitor has been looking back at me, watching as a boy who didn't know his ABCs turned into a young man who loved to write.

JULIA SAELEE, a member of the class of 2006, is attending UC Davis. Julie and her family are Mien from Laos.

In my sophomore year, I experienced something that I didn't anticipate. I thought it would be a day like any other, but my mundane bus ride home would be suddenly disrupted, and my sense of identity would never again be the same.

Every day I take a one-hour ride home, and I usually enjoy it because it gives me a chance to relax after a long day at school. But on this particular day, I felt uncomfortable as soon as I took my seat. As the bus headed towards my home, I could feel people staring at me. I remember becoming angry and embarrassed as a group of boys began to make perverse and explicitly degrading remarks about girls, especially Asian girls. Since I was the only Asian girl on the bus, I knew that they were targeting me. One boy began to chant the trite *"Ching chong"* stereotypical imitation of the Asian language. I wanted to run away at this point, but somehow I managed to stay on until I arrived at my stop. When I got home, I was at a loss about what to do, who to talk to, or how to feel. I felt ashamed and embarrassed because I was just humiliated and hadn't even defended myself.

A few weeks later, I had the chance to participate in Upward Bound's Annual Poetry Slam. My recollection of the incident on the bus still haunted me, so I decided if I wasn't able to speak up on the bus, I would now. Prior to this slam, I had never considered myself a poet, let alone imagined being a participant in a slam. The very thought of speaking in front of a large crowd was daunting. I remember shaking as I walked onstage. When I was in front of the microphone, I took a deep breath and began to tell my story. As I read each sentence, it felt as if I were redeeming myself and relieving embarrassment from the bus experience. I started out speaking slowly and calmly, but when my poem's tone changed and as I started to describe how I felt from the bus ride, I became less calm and spoke out angrily. I remember hearing my voice reverberate across the huge auditorium, piercing the silence and leaving some in the audience with a shocked expression. The sense of achievement that left me breathless that night is still with me today.

Although it was a relatively small slam, it was a supportive place to start, and I haven't stopped since then. I strive to inform others about my Mien culture through my poems and reach out to other girls who may have had similar experiences to mine and encourage them to speak out.

The following summer I participated in the same poetry slam. I was especially happy to see that I had inspired a younger friend of mine to participate also. I hope that her experience was as enriching as my own when she expressed herself in front of hundreds of people.

When I reflect back on that bus incident, I'm actually grateful that it happened. I was able to use it to my advantage and make a positive personal change. Without it I wouldn't have started to write and perform poetry and go through an eye-opening transformation.

Now, as a senior, I can see my transformation from being that quiet and passive girl in my sophomore year to the outspoken and confident person I am now.

JULIETTE JARDIM graduated from Berkeley High in 2004 and is currently a student at UCLA.

"*Bom dia,*" my professor says, interrupting herself and raising an eyebrow as I rush in 10 minutes late to my Portuguese class at Piedmont Adult School. "*Bom dia,*" I reply, smiling guiltily, a little out of breath and barely showered from water polo practice 30 minutes earlier in Berkeley, on the other side of the hills. I sit down in the front row and take my homework out as the teacher continues going over the difference between the verbs *ser* and *estar*. She speaks only in Portuguese, but I can follow the discussion. I'm a little more advanced than the rest of the class, which consists mainly of middle-aged men, searching for some means of communication with their Brazilian girlfriends.

As I repeat, "*Eu sou americana,*" I fidget with the raggedy, knotted red strings barely hanging on my wrist. The ribbon once said *Lem-*

brança do Senhor do Bonfim da Bahia, which means Souvenir of Our Lord of the Good Ending of Bahia. According to tradition, if one ties the ribbon with three knots, makes a wish for each knot and then wears the ribbon until it falls off, not only will the wishes come true, but the wearer will return to Brazil someday.

It's not surprising how easily I understand Portuguese. My father is of Portuguese descent, and my parents lived in Brazil for many years. Often I hear my parents' phone conversations with their numerous Brazilian friends or my dad's Portuguese relatives. In addition, my parents speak Portuguese when they want privacy, which is incentive enough for a kid to try to understand.

My parents met while teaching at an English school in São Paulo, Brazil. Later, they and their hippie friends moved to an island off the coast of Bahia, a state in the northeast of Brazil. Throughout my life, I've heard stories of their exotic island life with fire ants, tarantulas, and snakes that they killed and ate. As a little kid, this place was both horrifying and captivating.

When I finally visited this summer, I didn't eat any snakes, but I did experience firsthand what my parents love about Brazil: an unparalleled natural beauty, a multilayered mix of African, European, and indigenous cultures, and, the best part, Brazilians' warmth and friendliness. Encouraged and inspired to interact, I pulled together my French from school and limited knowledge of Portuguese and Spanish. By the end of my seven-week stay, I could understand most conversations, and in my slow, broken, Romance-language mix, I was able to communicate. I discussed Brazilian soap operas with a young couple during a layover at the airport, I taught some kids to play American card games on the beach, and I convinced a Capoeira (Brazilian martial art) student to demonstrate some of his moves.

Now, on top of daily water polo practice, flute lessons, church, fall lacrosse league, and coaching girls' lacrosse, I've found time for Portuguese. I want the conversations I started in Brazil to continue. Portuguese class is almost over. "*Estar* describes what you are now, it's transitive," explains my Portuguese professor. "*Ser* is constant, something you will always be."

I think, "*Eu estou nos Estados Unidos,* but at heart, *eu sou brasileira.*"

KIMIKO DIXON, a native of New Orleans, spent the fall semester of her senior year at Berkeley High School after losing everything during Hurricane Katrina. She returned to New Orleans in January of 2006.

Although my city has gone under, I realize that I am still standing. I am from New Orleans, and moved to California after losing my home as a result of Hurricane Katrina. This is the most difficult situation I have ever experienced, even more difficult than losing my mother at the age of nine. After my mother died, I turned to school as my way of dealing with grief. I have been a straight-A student since the sixth grade. I was on track to graduate as the valedictorian of my class at Edna Karr High School when Katrina struck. The transition has been extremely hard for me, not only because it is my senior year, but because I am without my family. In New Orleans, I lived with my grandparents and other close relatives, all in one house. Now our house, like most, is uninhabitable, and my family is living in a trailer in our driveway. When I left, I only had clothes for two days; I never thought that would be my last time going back to my house.

My grandfather, godmother, sister, and I retreated to a hotel to wait out the hurricane, while my grandmother, cousins, and uncle left the city. We spent three days in the hotel, on the 18th floor, after the hurricane passed, with no electricity or running water, and no communication with the outside world. It was not until we were evacuated from the hotel that we began to get an understanding of how extensive the damage was. Seeing the Superdome with two big holes in it, all the little babies dying and so many people trapped in their attics, forced me to realize that it was reality. Slowly, it became very clear that we would not be going back any time soon, but at the same time I was scared to think about where we would live. It was then that everyone decided that I should go to California with my godmother to finish school. I lost three weeks of school time before I started at Berkeley High, which is three times the size of my old school. I found it hard to socialize with the kids there. I was used to everyone having that "Southern hospitality," but that was not what I found. Instead, the kids treated me like a stranger who talked funny. At my old school, the new kids were asked questions and were welcomed into our circle, but at Berkeley High, I was ignored. Now the students are starting to talk to me more; however, just thinking of all the devastation and how much my family has lost is depressing and still makes me cry. This whole experience has given me previews of how college life will be, because I cannot run to my family and be comforted when I have a rough day: I often have to push myself to go the extra step, like my grandmother would push me. It has also made me put more value on my city and realize how influential my city is to the world and myself. Now I miss the culture of the city that could only be found in New Orleans.

LALITA KAEWSAWANG, a member of the Berkeley High class of 2006, came to Berkeley from Thailand when she was 13. Below are essays from three different college applications. She attends Wesleyan College.

AMHERST COLLEGE PROMPT

"Young as she is, the stuff of her life is a great cargo, and some of it heavy: I wish her a lucky passage." We are eager to know more about you. Your essays provide you with an opportunity to speak to us. Please keep this in mind when you respond to this quotation.

Many times in my life, I thought my education was over. After my younger sister was born, when I was a year old, our mother left us. Our father had a hard time finding a stable job or even knowing what he wanted to do. We were left with our grandmother, who had a business renting tricycles and a small farm where she grew bananas. She had no time for us, so we were placed in a child-care boarding house from nursery school through first grade. I often sat under a tree in the child-care house watching the gate to see if our grandma or our father would come to take my sister and me away.

Growing up, I heard my father and grandma argue about where to get money for us to go to school. In second grade, I shyly sold candy at school to help with money, until the principal called home to say I couldn't sell at school. Well, 1,000 baht, or $25, was made toward school, and the leftover candy was mine. Later, my father found a woman and a job owning a shop selling handcrafted wood items in the north, Chiang Mai. My sister and I moved up there with him, and I enrolled in fourth grade.

Sometimes my father and his girlfriend went out of town, and it was my responsibility to watch the shop and take care of my sister. When the dogs barked, the drunks crashed around, the wind banged on the window, no one was there for us. One experience in that shop that I will never forget was when one customer came in and ended up buying 100,000 baht, or $2,500, of furniture from me. It was hard. I had half of the prices in my head, and another half on a little piece of paper. I tried to be confident and mature. I did a good job, but it wasn't easy.

However, not very long after, my father broke up with his girlfriend, and his shop also broke down. That is when the next "stepmother" came along. She gave him a dream for a better future: his own house, new car, a new shop in Thailand, love for his children, and better education for us in the United States. I too was dreaming about what she offered and begged my father to come to America as soon as possible. His decision was made that he would send us here. The move did not turn out as she promised, but I am continuing my education.

COMMON APPLICATION, LONG ESSAY

At the age of 13, there was no one in my life I could trust. This was the year my father brought my younger sister and me to the United States. He stayed for a month and then went back to Thailand. We were left in Berkeley with his wife, a stepmother. She promised that we would have everything we didn't have in Thailand: a home, a mother, and love. Instead, she gradually gave us jobs to do at her restaurant. Before long, her restaurant became our home. My sister and I were forced to sleep in a dark room above the kitchen.

First, I worked for her as a favor because I thought it would pay her back for keeping us here. One day, I heard her say to her own children, "Aren't you happy? The girls are here to work for you, we just have to feed them." We ended up working seven nights a week from 5 to 11 p.m. without pay for four years. There wasn't a house or love to receive. Luckily, I was enrolled at Berkeley High School, where I found people whom I began to trust.

It took me four years to finally tell anyone about my situation. I had not wanted people to know about me before, because I really thought that without the stepmother, I would never survive in the United States. However, my desire for liberation and education were growing. I wanted to try. In my junior year I took a risk by sharing my story with my English teacher, Ms. W. I had just heard a college presentation from a counselor, and she had seen me cry. I didn't know then how important she would become to me, but she was the one who helped me begin to fight for my rights.

July 29, 2005, was Emancipation Day. A restraining order was served instead of our labor at five o'clock. My sister and I left the restaurant and moved in with Ms. W. This year is my first year to get out from the hard labor that has taken away my teenage life and interest. Now, I have an opportunity to put all my attention into school, taking more challenging courses and joining Youth and Government, the Y Scholars, and leading the Language and Culture Exchange Club. I have gained my freedom and learned to trust.

TUFTS UNIVERSITY PROMPT
"Education doesn't stretch your mind, if it doesn't force you to think about things in different ways . . . "

English is the key that changed my life. When I first came to the United States four years ago, I sat in the English classroom for English Language Learner students (ELL) and did not understand a single word. At the restaurant where I worked, I got in trouble with both customers and the stepfamily because I couldn't understand what they wanted or follow directions.

Learning English changed my perception of people. The stepmother had treated me condescendingly when I could not pronounce English words correctly, when I didn't know the meaning of the Fourth of July, or ordered wrong foods. At school, I found people who were understanding of my mistakes, helped me pronounce words correctly and learn new traditions. I realized that was a better way of treating people than my stepmother did. By my junior year I knew enough English to tell my story in detail and to understand words from others as if English were my birth language. I can now communicate, share feelings and thoughts, and that is important.

Once I knew English, I knew what the stepmother did wasn't right. I gained the strength and confidence to escape from the stepmother and the initiative to fight for what I wanted to be.

LAUREN SILVERMAN, a member of the Berkeley High class of 2006, is a student at the University of Michigan.

Freshman year I was admitted into Stanford Hospital with an eating disorder.

I didn't starve myself to be thin; let's get that straight. I felt lost freshman year, I was struggling to find my niche among the other students in my school, and I turned to the only variable I felt I could control: food. I was performing a disappearing act, but at first people didn't notice I was vanishing. Looking back, it's clear I was headed in the wrong direction, but when I was caught in the middle of it, I didn't know how to get help. Finally, I told my parents I was ready to check into the hospital, and thankfully, I quickly regained my health and was released after less than a month.

As I walked outside of the hospital, I embraced the fresh air along with the challenge of recovery, despite all of the statistics not in my favor. Much harder than gaining weight was the realization that I had lost friends through the whole experience, that people I met the first few months of high school might remember me as someone of whom I was not proud.

I decided to do something about my shame, to share my experience on the radio in hopes of shedding light on the misconceptions of eating disorders. Since I was an intern at Youth Radio in Berkeley, I had access to a recording studio but no idea whether some anonymous editor would broadcast my story, shoot it down, or rework it for years. I pitched my radio essay, and an editor ripped it to shreds, but I still felt compelled to write about anorexia, a subject I hadn't heard talked about from a youth's perspective on the radio before. With each digital edit I made on the computer, I wanted to go back in my life and cut out the parts I was disappointed with, to replace them with my triumphs, but I couldn't go back in time. Instead, I let my past ride the airwaves, positive that my success story would provide encouragement for others, or at least offer a voice for those too uncomfortable to share their own.

Last summer I was awarded a Gracie Allen Award by the American Women in Radio and Television for my commentary. The organization AWRT celebrates national programming created by women. The honor meant a great deal, but more important was knowing that people were acknowledging my voice.

Two years and many revisions later, my commentary went from local radio stations to National Public Radio's Morning Edition. Millions of people heard my personal narrative that morning, and with each person I ran into who mentioned my radio story, my shame diminished and was replaced with pride.

I didn't realize it at first, but I now see that the microphone didn't simply enlarge the sound waves of my voice; it enlarged my sense of self and obligation to my community. Long ago the obsessive part of me left, and in the years since my recovery I am grateful that I have learned how to turn obstacles into opportunities to grow.

GEORGE WASHINGTON UNIVERSITY PROMPT
As you strive further in your education, we are interested in knowing what matters most to you. Tell us how an experience you have had, an interest you have pursued, or a person you have known shaped your thinking.

Minutes after the lunch bell rang, I stepped into my first Black Student Union meeting. Only days before, I had heard the club was "open to everyone," but I soon found out that didn't mean everyone came.

A week before there had been a brainstorming meeting with some leaders from the Black Student Union (BSU) and the editors of the *Jacket,* the Berkeley High School newspaper, on how to diversify the paper so that it could more accurately represent the student body. Many of the editors, myself included, were aware that the *Jacket* wasn't perfect, but believed it covered issues relevant to all of the students at our school. My assumptions were struck down as Rico, a classmate and leader of BSU, talked about being stopped in the halls, and the lack of college information in the black community, topics not mentioned in the paper. Rico forced me to examine my belief that my high school experience was generic, that it applied to everyone, like some sort of boring TV show. Rico had suggested some editors from the *Jacket* stop by the BSU meeting. Excited, I marked Wednesday's meeting date in my planner, but come lunchtime no one else wanted to join me, and I kept asking myself, "Why I am doing this?" I knew I was there for more than the school newspaper; I was there to collaborate with a new group of people.

So, there I was, sticking out like a bleach stain in the dark wash, but I stayed seated. I feared that the unfamiliar faces in the BSU might call me out as the only white person in the room, or even request I leave— but they didn't. By the end of lunch no one had touched their food, but the whiteboard was quilted with different people's ideas for diversifying the paper. "Presenting to English classes, giving applications to different ethnic clubs on campus . . . " I was stunned when I raised my hand, and one of my ideas went up along with my peers' contributions.

I stayed late talking to Sherick, the president, whom I knew from soccer and dance, and with a little encouragement I became an official member of the BSU. Looking back on this year, AP Calculus may have taxed my mind the most with derivatives and integrals, but BSU meetings opened my mind to problems unsolvable by any one formula—just the way I like it.

LAUREN SONDEREGGER graduated in 2005. She is a student at Yale University.

My favorite swimming pool has no walls, chlorine, nor tile. The Golden Gate Bridge and the enclosing coastline define its limits, and Alcatraz and Angel Island are my starting blocks. This unique swimming pool is San Francisco Bay, a curiously shaped expanse of choppy teal-brown water of mysterious content, ranging in temperature from 45 to 70 degrees Fahrenheit.

As a 13-year-old, I had only known competitive pool swimming. One day, a coach on my swim team enticed me to miss the first half of a grueling workout with tales of an unusual place to swim, where seals might attack me and I would reek for days after. "How intriguing," I thought, and followed my older teammates down to the Berkeley Marina for my first "Bay swim."

Since then, I've participated in this unusual sport several times a month, all throughout the year, as a respite from ordinary pool swimming. Faithful to our routine, my teammates and I jump shrieking off the old, dilapidated pier at the Marina, anticipating the cold shock of the salty water and the ensuing rush of excitement and adrenaline. (I've been nicknamed "Shark-bait" because I always plunge first into the deep.) Swimming out west into the setting sun around the bayside restaurant and toward the Berkeley Pier, we battle the choppy waves and imagine in fear all the unknown creatures that lurk on the muddy floor of the Bay. We wave at the early diners in the restaurant and always get a laugh out of what they must be thinking when they see a few crazy swimmers passing by. Even after four years of swimming in this chilly water, no matter how unpleasant my day has been, or how stressed out I am, a frigid swim in the Bay has been, without fail, a great pick-me-up.

In addition to being purely for fun, our Bay adventures serve as preparation for numerous open-water races. My personal favorite is the "Alcatraz Swim," a chilly 2,000-yard crossing from Alcatraz Island to Aquatic Park in San Francisco that I have completed 10 times since I was 14. Almost 1,000 people wake up while it's still dark on a Saturday morning to board a ferry and share the anticipation of jumping into circa-58-degree water, still shrouded in fog. Whether you're wearing a two-inch thick wetsuit as protection from the cold, or braving the elements as a "naked" swimmer like my teammates and me, everyone is proud of participating in this crazy feat. I thrive on the emphasis on the *process and experience* of the race. I come away from Alcatraz swims feeling inspired, refreshed, and salty, ready to tackle all that life might throw in my way. After all, I have the courage, stamina, and desire to numb my extremities for the better part of an hour to do what generations of convicts could only dream of. Consequently, I am usually confident when taking an intimidating exam, and have the courage to stand by my convictions.

Another special aspect of Bay swimming for me is the connection with nature. More than once I've stopped during an Alcatraz race and looked around at the gorgeous sight of the rising sun reflecting on San Francisco. I'm overcome with the glorious feeling that I'm all alone out there in the Bay, simply because those 1,000 swimmers are hopelessly scattered on such an impressive expanse of water. I marvel at how utterly tiny I am in comparison with the enormous mass of water around me, and experience a sense of uneasiness that I love—for even though this vastness of water is my friend and teacher, it could just as easily kill me with its temperatures, tides, and creatures.

Bay swimming refreshes me and brightens my day with its mix of thrill and marvelous uneasiness. To think that I sometimes *pay* to see creepy movies to conjure that unmistakable feeling of suspense and apprehension! More often I just go for an awesome swim in my favorite swimming pool, San Francisco Bay.

LIAM SMITH graduated from Berkeley High in 2005. He attends Ursinus College in Pennsylvania.

Last summer my father was trying to revive a bankrupt landscape supply company, Acapulco Rock and Soil. Every day new debts would come to light, and the bookkeeper turned out to be an embezzler. The company was struggling just to keep its day-to-day operations going; but, miraculously, sales continued to be good. Summer was the busiest time, and, although my dad was reluctant to add to the payroll, the manager couldn't handle all the business by himself. He needed an assistant. After the corrupt bookkeeper, they wanted to hire someone who was trustworthy, above all. In addition, the new hire would have to be able to add in his head, and learn how to operate the computer programs, plus absorbing everything there was to know about rocks and soil. He would have to be able to sell by weight or volume, and do all of this in both Spanish and English. Not surprisingly, no one who fit this description could be found, especially at the wages they were willing to pay, so my dad asked me.

Naively, I agreed. I was excited about starting at Acapulco because it gave me an opportunity to gain real-world experience and have a taste of the responsibilities that most people face every day.

When I arrived on my first day I was amazed; it was only 7:45 in the morning and the yard was already buzzing. Rafino and Alfredo, the forklift operators, were loading pallets of rocks onto pickup trucks, while landscapers patrolled the yard trying to find the perfect rock (to the trained eye each rock really is unique, I soon learned). My job was to help the manager, JB, keep this chaos running smoothly. Soon I was figuring out the accounting program, while trying to serve customers as quickly and competently as possible, since at this hour they were all eager to reach their job sites. It took all of my presence of mind to enter sales correctly, identify the materials, and answer questions thrown at me by the customers, many of whom spoke only Spanish.

When the morning rush ended, I was ready for a break, but JB took me out into the yard for a crash course in rocks and soil. For instance, I learned not to sell people sand to put between their brick pavers, because, although it holds them together better than any other material, it washes away with the first rain. The right material for the job is finely crushed gravel called decomposed granite, or DG. What I later learned was that DG, like many of the materials we sold, had at least three other names in English, and a few more Spanish ones.

One of the things JB liked about me was that I was able to retain this kind of information, and he only had to tell me things once. By the third day I knew enough about the products and I could work the computer well enough for JB to leave me to run the business by myself while he got lunch. At first it was nerve-wracking to be on my own. But, after I was able to resolve problem after problem by myself, I became confident in my ability to handle just about anything that could come up, even if I had to improvise. By the end of summer I was working full shifts as manager by myself.

I have always had an ability to think on my feet, but after my time at

Acapulco I feel that I have the confidence to apply this ability in chaotic and intimidating situations that might have scared me before. I believe this quality will help me make the best use of the intellectual training that I hope to acquire, and will stand me in good stead both at college and in the world beyond it.

LIZA RUZER, a member of the Berkeley High class of 2004, is a student at Clark University.

My family and I waited nine years for permission to emigrate from Russia. In 1991, we were given 10 days to pack our belongings and leave. We settled in Berkeley, where I was enrolled in kindergarten. On the first day I wore shoes and clothes donated by the Jewish Family and Children's Services, including my first pair of sneakers. In Russia my only shoes had been a pair of functional yet unremarkable boots. The sneakers were the most beautiful shoes I had ever seen, with three shades of pink and white laces. I proudly walked to my first day of school thinking that everyone would admire them. To my surprise, no one noticed. I didn't understand why all my classmates didn't crowd around me. Surely in my old neighborhood everyone would have. I realized that things were different in this new country.

Coming to America brought other significant changes. For the first time, my family and I were allowed to practice our religion freely. My family joined a nearby synagogue that we still attend today. I was enrolled in the synagogue's Hebrew School and attended its summer camp. The fight my parents endured to live in a country where we could practice our religion freely makes me appreciative of the opportunities and freedoms that I have today. The religious freedom came at a cost, however. Things were very different outside of my family, and my parents worked hard to retain the Russian culture at home. I was given spelling tests and practiced reading and writing in Russian. I celebrate Russian New Year with a tree, am able to cherish movies my parents grew up on, and can appreciate *Catcher in the Rye* in both English and Russian. The greatest impact on my family, however, has been the financial struggle. I was jealous of my friends who spent their parents' money frivolously on clothes and makeup. Today I work three days a week behind the front desk at a yoga studio. I have also been babysitting two children since freshman year. Their mom takes night classes and is unable to drive me home because she is a single parent, so after babysitting I take an hour-long bus ride home. The money I make helps me pay for clothing, public transportation, and most of my food. I come home exhausted from the long day and must stay up late to finish my homework. At school, not many people realize what I am going through. Just as no one noticed my sneakers, not many people understand that I must work in order to persevere. I have come a long way from the day my family arrived in America. I am grateful for my experiences as an immigrant, and I can look back and see that my hard work has taught me a lot about the world. Starting from scratch has been both financially and emotionally hard, but the progress my family has made since our arrival proves that the work has paid off.

MARI MONOSOFF-RICHARDS graduated from Berkeley High in 2007 and has decided to attend Oberlin College in Ohio.

"Push, send, push, send, let's take a p-o-w-e-r ten in three, two, one. Ready! TEN, NINE, EIGHT!" My coxswain urges us on in her gravelly voice. She encourages us to push as hard as we can, give all our energy so we can pass the boat next to us before reaching the last 500-meter mark. I'm more charged than the rest because I'm the first to pass the end of our opponent's boat.

I loved crew. With crew there was little other life—three-hour practices, six practices a week (up to eight in racing season), and a race on the seventh day. To commit two years of my life to this schedule showed devotion I wasn't aware I possessed. I loved my team, my coach, the boats, and I loved gliding fast over the water. My friends voted me most likely to compete in the Olympics. Small for a rower, my passion surpassed my size. I loved racing.

Then, during sophomore year, I felt stabbing pain in both knees. I didn't want to stop, but my coach began to pull me out of boats during practice, unwilling to watch me wince. I couldn't enjoy the synchronization of rowing with eight other people. Still I finished the season with the mentality of "one more row can't hurt me."

Junior year, I thought about attending the crew meeting. I missed the endorphins and excitement, but I was already busy. My friend, the technical director of Berkeley High's theater, had learned that the women who normally costumed our school shows were unavailable. I found myself in the theater's costume room with a script and the instructions, "Costumes! Laramie Project! GO!" As with crew, I spent many long hours, and with some guidance, I filled my orders. Twenty-three actors, 57 characters, 184 shirts, shoes, jackets, and ties paraded onstage, showing off my hard work. Besides learning how to costume a show, I learned traditional aspects of technical theater like set design and sound. On many occasions I balanced myself atop of a tall ladder, reaching above my head to hang and focus lights.

Opening night was incredible. I wasn't onstage, but I was right behind it. I sat backstage and helped with countless five-second changes. Not only did I get to hear the powerful speeches made by the characters, but I also saw how the words impacted the actors. I was the spectator of two shows. As the cast and crew bonded, I became part of a new family. From being hooked on endorphins, I became hooked on theater.

It's thrilling to find a talent in an unknown area and wonderful to be reassured that there is much more in life to be discovered. I became passionate about theater. I love the process where strangers become friends. I miss crew, but I have a new team now.

MELEIA WILLIS-STARBUCK graduated from Berkeley High in 2003. She completed two years at Dartmouth College before she was tragically shot and killed on a Berkeley street in the summer of 2005. At the time she was working in a women's shelter.

I slid my nails across the speckled table and down the leg. My fingernails tapped against the cold metal as I sat in my seventh-period chemistry class waiting for the first bell to ring. My eyes rolled towards the clock. The minute hand, after what seemed like hours, finally reached the six. *Briiiiiiiiiiing.* Once the rest of the class settled, our teacher rose from his chair. After removing his hands from his pockets, he proceeded to speak. "Welcome to the first day of the second semester. I'm sure you all have noticed that we have lost a few of our students." Half of the class was missing, to be exact. The students who had failed consisted of all the minorities with the exception of myself and a few Asian students. "It's unfortunate, but a lot of them just couldn't cut it. After all, they earned the grades they received." He continued to talk to the class about our lost group of students, but I forced myself to stop listening.

A high failure rate for minorities is one of the many effects of the achievement gap that Berkeley High School is so famously known for.

Traces of the achievement gap can be found in places other than the classroom. When lunch is over and the first bell rings, signaling everyone to return to class, all the white students pack up their belongings and walk toward their classes, while black and brown students continue to mingle amongst their peers.

Although I have a diverse group of friends, my immediate social circle is predominantly black. Like the majority of African American students at Berkeley High, they too don't attend class regularly or on time. Forcing myself not to hang out with my associates after lunch has ended and fourth period has begun requires a lot of willpower. As a result I have been forced to learn at an early age that it is important to surround myself with those who succeed, and sometimes this means leaving people behind.

However, constantly succeeding without my black and brown friends is far from a solution. I have decided that I am going to take a more proactive stance on this problem that has been plaguing Berkeley High for a number of decades. I am well known for my involvement in many campus organizations and extracurricular activities. I have used this to my advantage. Whether I'm fulfilling my role as the Black Student Union president, a peer health educator, or the president of the Honor Society, I bring awareness to achievement gap–related issues.

During my sophomore year I served as a member of the board of directors for a youth-run organization titled African American Latino Leadership (AALL). We began to tackle achievement gap–related issues that the Berkeley School Board hadn't even begun to discuss. We created mentor groups, provided tutoring, and hosted events that connected minority families. For all this awareness, however, I have yet to devise an effective and appropriate way to confront the snide remarks of a teacher proud to have gotten rid of the minority students in his class. I plan on working on it during the remainder of my education.

MOLLIE SCHOENWALD **graduated in 2005 and is currently a student at Northwestern University.**

NORTHWESTERN UNIVERSITY PROMPT
In 1972, Edward Lorenz theorized that a butterfly flapping its wing in Brazil could cause a tornado in Texas. What small action had a larger impact than you expected? How were you affected by the consequences?

I tentatively opened the door to Room C113 on the first day of my freshman year, to be greeted by Mrs. Karla Herndon, whose unassuming paisley sundress and calm demeanor was merely a show for the freshman, she made sure to tell us. Majestically perched on her rickety stool, hands folded in her lap, she suddenly burst into song: *"Eram, eras, erat, eramus, eratis, erant,"* to the tune of the Mexican Hat Dance. Soon the entire class put aside their nervousness and joined her in singing. Already I knew that she was no ordinary teacher.

C113 was my escape from the pandemonium of Berkeley High School. There, Mrs. Herndon gave us the key that revealed the buried world of Virgil, Caesar, Livy, Cicero, Ovid, and made it come alive. As we gazed up at Mrs. Herndon during her lectures, I could hear the bustle of senators rushing through the Forum, I could discern Cicero standing at the Rostra declaring the guilt of audacious Catiline, I could sense the tension of a country on the brink of civil war. She led me far beyond the fourth declension or the passive periphrastic; she led me into the daily lives of the Roman people—their architecture, culture, habits, and literature.

I did not fully understand where Mrs. Herndon was guiding me until one foggy day in February of my junior year. With the smell of Mrs. Herndon's cauliflower lunch still lingering in the air, the Latin class trickled into C113. Some excited, some lethargic, we sat down to translate the *Aeneid*. My revelation came as we read the passage in which

Aeneas and his comrades encounter a ferocious storm at sea. Mrs. Herndon lectured on timelessness, on the immortality of Virgil's characters, on the larger-than-life situations, on the moral lessons contained in the text, which have as much relevance today as in Virgil's time. From beneath her lovingly worn text, she pulled out a letter written by her father during his service on a battleship in World War II. As she read this letter, her voice never faltered: Instead, her intensity heightened with every crashing wave and pounding surf—emotions and scenes depicted exactly like those that we had translated only minutes before. It clicked. The parallels of the two storm scenes blossomed in my mind, recalling the disregard for human life during times of war. Even more broadly, I saw the connection between the *Aeneid* and modern struggles, both national and personal. This realization of historical continuity overwhelmed me. At that moment I knew my fate as a Classics major had been sealed: *Iacta alea est,* the die has been cast.

Molly Stewart-Cohn, a member of the Berkeley High class of 2004, was accepted early decision at Vassar.

The tradition in the theater department of my school is to allow the technical staff to take a bow on closing night. After the actors have gone through the motions of curtain call, the techies file onstage, hands linked, to make our bow, before stepping upstage. I always downplay the importance that taking the bow has to me (after all, what would a true techie care about being seen on stage?) yet in reality, this brief interlude in the otherwise actor-reserved space is one of the highlights of any school show.

Why I feel this way is a mystery. I certainly don't desire to be an actor; I have a long list of reasons why I find technical work preferable. The stage itself is not an unknown territory. I do a large amount of work on it, whether it be focusing lights or repairing cables or moving sets into place. Yet when the house is filled with people, their faces indistinguishable but obviously turned in your direction, the uncomfortably warm lights shining in your eyes, the stage is suddenly a different realm, one normally left exclusively for the actors.

Perhaps I have some buried dramatic spark that urges me toward performance, nourished by my theatrical family and a childhood of Shakespeare plays and Broadway musicals, which lends me a fondness for extravagant hand gestures or prompts me to make flamboyant bows after performing scene changes even though nobody can see me. More likely, I simply relish the acknowledgment of my work that a closing-night bow gives me. For weeks the technicians work behind the scenes, devote their lunchtimes to building scenery, and come in extra days to focus lights so that the first day actors arrive at the theater, everything is, almost magically, ready for them. On closing night, actors step aside for a moment to let the techies take center stage, and, for once, the audience sees evidence of the invisible people responsible for all the little theatrical miracles, the lights and sounds and sets, that transform a show from a bunch of teenagers reciting memorized lines to a real place and story the audience can get lost in. After all my hard work, I get to leave my post, walk onstage, and receive a moment of clapping and a word of thanks.

This year I've been promoted to co-head of the tech crew and lighting designer. Consequently, I've spent the last few weeks holding one-sided conversations with my friends about the merits of purple light over green. I've been indulging the overly organized, mathematical side of my personality by fantasizing about how to logically arrange the other techies to most efficiently hang and focus the lights. I relish the opportunity to run the crew in a more professional, coordinated way than before, when nobody really had an assigned task. Yet, secretly, I look forward to closing night, when I will not only get to bow, but will be acknowledged for the first time by name, and I'll step forward to receive a bouquet of flowers.

NOAH FINE NATHEL graduated in 2005 and is a student at Cornell University.

My family loves food. When we're not eating, we're talking about eating. My parents always fed me relatively healthy foods (with the occasional Oreo thrown in). I ate whatever was there, and never thought much about it. Then I learned intriguing information about nutrition and health, and nothing has been the same for me since.

For example: Certain porous fruits soak up pesticides to a concentration that is dangerous. Strawberries and peanuts are profoundly affected. So, unless the peanuts were grown organically, that good old PB&J—lovingly packed off to school as a "healthy lunch"—is anything but healthy. Call me weird but, when I was 14, the irony of this had me spellbound.

My interest in health started even earlier. When I was 11, I picked up a children's book about diseases. I remember that its tone was perversely cheery. The diseases were alphabetized, and I quickly became engaged in the section on cancer (Look under "C"!), no doubt experiencing a touch of hypochondriasis (Look under "H"!). Later, in biology class, I became enthralled with the genetic process, and how the smallest aberration could result in a life-threatening disease.

After the strawberry-peanut epiphany, I began to pay closer attention to ingredient labels—but recognized that I wasn't exactly living the healthiest lifestyle. Like many kids, I'm massively sleep-deprived. When I'm wiped out after an all-nighter, it wouldn't matter whether my diet were certified organic or comprised entirely of Snickers and Mountain Dew. I've addressed this common problem by starting an "Insomnia

Club" at school (where kids can learn about the importance of sleep, and even catch a wink during meetings). Nutrition is vital, but so is a healthy lifestyle.

I want a broad undergraduate education, but I'd definitely like to do some disease-related research in college—something like Professor Folkman's work on angiogenesis inhibitors that starve tumors of blood they need to grow, or maybe even something of my own on the nutrition-lifestyle-cancer connection. After college, I want to go to medical school and then specialize in oncology. Like many people considering a medical career, I've been wondering how I'll handle the emotional part of working with real patients. So I became a volunteer at a home for terminally ill children. At first, the facility seemed like Eden. I read the popular children's story *Frog and Toad* to a young patient there. Then I got an e-mail from the administrator that she had died.

I've learned facts and empirical data about diet and lifestyle issues that inspire me and that have led me to make changes to improve my health. I know how fortunate I am to have so many compelling learning opportunities ahead of me. I relish my luck, and become even more earnest about practicing oncology whenever I remember the irony of reading *Frog and Toad*—an allegory about life lessons—to a girl who will never get the chance to apply them.

OSCAR ROJAS-SOTO graduated in 2004 and is currently a student at UC Berkeley. He returns on a regular basis to Berkeley High to work at the Student Learning Center, an after-school tutoring program.

My father came to the United States in 1990, and later brought my family to the United States in 1991 when I was three, my brother one, and my sister a newborn. We came to this country in order to establish a better life, and in many ways I can honestly say this country has offered my family many opportunities, even though my parents' "American Dream" did not turn out exactly as they had planned.

When we arrived, my parents struggled to find employment that would pay a decent wage. While my parents were seeking stable and adequate jobs, my family moved from place to place and stayed with family and friends. Finally, when I was eight, we were able to find a two-bedroom house of our own. Our home was in one of the roughest neighborhoods of East Oakland, where there are drug dealers just around the corner, where three of my bikes were stolen, and where my uncle and some family friends were assaulted in broad daylight. As ironic as it sounds, it was nice to find a place that we could call our own.

Although our housing situation stabilized, our economic situation soon took a downturn when my dad's health worsened due to an accident he had a couple of years earlier in work that injured his back. After having a couple of operations, he developed rheumatoid arthritis. This left him unable to work, and it was up to my mother to find a job that would support the household. The constant stress of working, while still trying to manage a household and take care of my father, slowly began to take a toll on my mother's emotional health. She always looked tired and overworked, so I tried to help her as much as I could by taking care of my younger siblings. As the years passed, she became more and more emotionally unstable and constantly felt depressed. Once I was in high school, I remember neither parent was able to work at a steady job. It was around that time that we began receiving notices that we would be evicted if we couldn't pay the rent.

Eventually, after finding it impossible to make ends meet, my parents decided it would be best to return to Mexico. My siblings and I were confused; we didn't not know where we fell into their plan. We could not imagine having to leave all of our friends and go live in a country we hardly knew. Knowing that it would be hard for us to make a transition to life in Mexico, and still wanting at least the children to take advantage of the opportunities in the United States, my parents told us that my siblings and I would stay in the United States with another family, while my parents would go back to Mexico.

By late 2001, my parents had already left for Mexico, and my siblings and I were under the care of Luis and Carmen Baez. We were devastated by the sudden separation of our family; however, our legal guardians were very supportive and stimulated us to do well in school, even though neither of them had had the opportunity to finish high school. It was during this period of my life that I really became interested in religion. Carmen and Luis stimulated us to read and study the Bible, which came to be a consolation and aid to us in overcoming the sadness of being separated from our parents. Another way that I dealt with the situation was by succeeding academically. I became very active in school and concentrated on my work in order to keep my mind busy and to help deal with the hardship of not having my parents close to me.

Another way that I dealt with these issues was by becoming very involved in the community around me. I joined several clubs and organizations, such as TOJIL, Kids Care International, and La Raza Unida. I realize how, even though I had gone through a lot in my life, there were still other underprivileged youth who had gone through worse obstacles in life than me. And I wanted to help them do well in life, either by keeping them off the streets and doing positive activities, or by educating them about their ancestral roots and their history.

I was officially adopted in March of 2003. Only three months later, my stepdad died of a heart attack. This also was a tough period of my life; I dealt with it by keeping myself busy with schoolwork, and working to help out my family economically. If I had the opportunity to attend a University of California, I could become better prepared to help those around me and in my community to also do well in life.

RACHEL ORKIN-RAMEY graduated from Berkeley High School in 1997 and from Amherst College in 2001. She is currently working at Christie's in London.

Connie Pearlstein always reminded me of a big, dark crow, swooping across the yard or the classroom. When you're five years old, the details dominate the picture, so I have an interesting slant on what I remember of my kindergarten teacher from that year. Connie (everyone called her Connie) had a deep, booming voice, heavy black eyebrows, and she stood a mile high. She always wore wool. These are the physical characteristics that I remember: tall and wool. The wool part is important—she always wore wool pants, long wool sweaters that she had knitted, and big coats that flapped around her. She was imposing, but we adored her.

I'm not sure why the others loved her, but I loved her because she made me feel important. She talked without condescension, even if we deserved to be condescended to. Connie stood firm amid the chaos, while we hung onto her pants. All we could reach were her knees, but we wanted to hold her. When she read to us, which was anytime she could, kids held onto her like a security blanket. Connie loved books fiercely and deeply, and so we also loved them. She would check books out of the school library, huge stacks, taller than I was, and so many that the librarian got angry. Connie is one reason why for me, many things rank a distant second to a good book.

In spite of all this, I doubt that would have influenced me as much had she not kept in touch with me. I know no other people who still talk to their kindergarten teachers. She calls several times a year, and every time, she starts by saying, "Hello, Rach, this is Connie Pearlstein." She drawls out her name, so the first syllable of "Connie" takes as much time to say as the rest of her name. She is the only person I have ever let call me "Rach," even when I was young and my full name was a mouthful. Her manner of treating me as a friend carries over to this day, when I get packages from her addressed to "Friend Rachel."

I am expecting two books of Greek and Roman plays from her. One, she said, is a little battered. She kicked it across the field at Scripps after a particularly bad day in class. She still pushes books and articles on me, although now I'm an eager recipient. She does the same thing with her grandchildren. She says, "When they get a present from Grams, they know it's a book."

When Connie taught me, she was commuting several hours from Pacific Grove to Berkeley. The five daughters she had raised by herself had grown up and left home. She retired when I was in first grade and now she lives in Pacific Grove full-time. I remember her house—warm, dark, crowded with piles of books and knitting. (Some things change, but the wool remains the same.) She said that her house was haunted. I think that if Connie had been architecture, she would have been a cottage, with books and cats and armchairs. A place I'd like to live in.

**ROBERT REYNOLDS graduated in 2005
and attends UC Santa Cruz.**

"Youth aren't ready for the vote," my friend said.

"Of course we are," I answered.

"Why?" she asked in a serious tone.

"To be represented by the system, we need to vote," I replied, inspired by an Internet article about a youth gathering signatures to lower Florida's voting age. "If politicians had to worry about earning our vote, they would spend more money on schools."

"Kids are ignorant of current events!"

"Adults aren't tested to see how well informed they are on the issues.

Knowledge of the issues has nothing to do with the right to vote. The question is, do we have interests that only we can be the best judge of? And because I believe we do, I believe we should have the right to express those interests on a ballot."

Silence.

"Wouldn't kids vote for MTV musicians and movie stars?"

"Who voted for Arnold Schwarzenegger?" I ask, wearing an expanding smile because I know I have her.

The Progressive Club at Berkeley High School started innocuously in October 2003, with me wandering the halls pinning up announcements. As founder and president, I suggested our first event, which turned out to be enormously conspicuous—a polling place picket during the 2004 presidential primary against youth disenfranchisement.

Our message, represented on signs like "Got Ballots, I Need One," "Lower the Voting Age!" and "No Taxation Without Representation!" among others, put us in several major newspapers. Over the next few weeks I was amazed to see my name emblazoned in the *Boston Globe,* the *San Francisco Chronicle*, the *Oakland Tribune*, the *San Jose Mercury News*, and the *Daily Californian*. I was even "Teen of the Month" in Japan's largest daily newspaper, *Yomiuri Shimbun.*

There were also dozens of online articles (put "Robert Reynolds voting age" in your favorite search engine to see what I mean). For a while, the phone rang off the hook with interview requests from television and radio stations.

In Washington, D.C., the president of the National Youth Rights Association (NYRA), a seven-year-old youth-rights-advocacy group, read about our protest and sent us messages of support. We found that NYRA had a growing membership, with members in cities from Los Angeles to New York City and from Seattle to Miami, and that they were devoted to building a base of support for the youth-rights movement, so our club joined and became the Berkeley chapter.

I have become extremely active in the organization. I ran for the board of directors and won, and since then the board has elected me to be national vice president. I know it is a small organization, but I take my responsibility as vice president quite seriously.

My activism has stimulated discussions with my friends and others, and while I really enjoy debate, I've come to feel a kinship with other civil-rights pioneers—like Susan B. Anthony, Malcolm X, and Martin Luther King, Jr., who were ahead of popular opinion but worked against overwhelming odds for what they saw as just and fair.

I feel that the most effective way to counter those who oppose youth rights is to learn their arguments, and use what I know to find new ways of helping them look at the issue. I have already begun my political career on a small level. In addition to NYRA and the Progressive Club, I have been involved in the PTSA, the Model United Nations, the Berkeley School Board, and the Building with Books Club, an organization dedicated to raising money to build schools in Third World countries. I intend to study law and eventually pursue a career in politics.

Sarah True, a member of the class of 2007, was accepted early decision at Barnard College.

BARNARD COLLEGE PROMPT
Indicate a person who has had a significant influence on you and describe that influence.

I step onto the hard dirt road. A warm breeze from Lake Victoria blows my hair across my grinning face. My hands smell of paint. My group and I arrived in Africa after four months of intense fund-raising and have just finished painting a mural on the walls of the hospital in

Shirati, Tanzania. Turning from a large dirt road with potholes the size of elephants onto a small dirt path with potholes the size of mere warthogs, I start the walk home. I pass clay, thatch-roofed huts and nonchalantly step over a rope connecting the horns of a bull to a bush. It is my fourth week in Shirati, and avoiding roaming cows, goats, and chickens has become second nature. As I pass Mama Baraka's house of 15 orphans I pause and scan for my favorite little girl, the girl who has a piece of my heart. I don't see her and walk on with my shoulders slumped. But sure enough, an ecstatic smile stretches across my face when the familiar footsteps pitter-patter on the path behind me. I turn to see Nema racing toward me, barefoot, clumsily ignoring the rocks and holes, running with as much grace as a four-year-old can.

As she dashes toward me I question why I get a roof over my head, running water, a bed, and health care, why I get a free education and complain about homework when Nema may never set foot in a classroom. Because I came to Shirati to teach kids about HIV, it's ironic that this little girl, orphaned by AIDS, is teaching me so much about life. Spending time with her every day brings home to me the dismal conditions that my friends here experience daily. Nema makes me realize that although it is just one month and just one child, doing what I can to make this one child feel special is making a difference. She makes me realize that I am taking small steps to make a life valued. As I will pursue a career in international public health, these steps will continue to a place where I can influence people to treat a deprived African child not just as a sad statistic, but as a girl who is as important as I am. In doing this, I hope that I can leave Nema with more than a piece of my heart and a new pair of shoes.

Now I see that my smile is mirrored on her face, and the shine in her eye, I know, is mirrored in mine. A few feet away, she takes her final leap into my arms, and I pull her into an embrace and begin to tickle her, just to hear her soft, seldom-heard laugh. As always, I lose myself in this moment, when we can forget our troubles, that she is one of 15 orphans of AIDS, she doesn't own a pair of shoes, she can't go to school because she can't afford a uniform, and she may not have eaten today. When I swing her around we know that even for this short amount of time, we are special to each other.

Sascha Atkins-Loria graduated from Berkeley High in 2004. She is a student at Vassar College. Common Ground, the program she joined sophomore year at BHS, no longer exists.

My auntie and my mama don't like white people, Patrice tells me. Hot air blows through the windows of our freshman English classroom, and my skin burns. Patrice keeps talking. *Me, I like white people. They cool.* I look up at her quickly and she laughs loudly to disguise her discomfort. Am I nothing but another white face, my flaws and quirks irrelevant because of my color? I blink quickly to lock the stinging frustration inside my eyes.

Did you ever think that all white people aren't the same? I ask her slowly. Patrice shrugs, looks down at her own dark skin, and then pulls out an assignment we are working on together.

Go ahead, work, she orders. The bell rings as I glare at the paper she points to, and I push my way through too many desks out into a mess of people stumbling down the hallway.

I don't blame Patrice; it was her attempt to compensate for the prejudice of her family that led her to tell me she likes "white people." It is not my place to be angry, and Patrice's comment is what I must accept as a result of the tears her auntie and mama must have shed. Their tears are not my fault, but they have become mine to carry, and I know I shouldn't complain about the load.

At the end of freshman year, I decide to join Common Ground, a diverse program focusing on environmental and social change. However painful and heavy others' tears are to carry, I would rather bear that weight than join the mostly white, upper-middle-class students as they separate themselves from the diversity of Berkeley High into the AP track. I am taking hard classes of a different sort, because I believe there is much to learn through experience.

♦ ♦ ♦

It is sophomore year, and we sit in a Common Ground U.S. history class. Pictures of President Hoover slide across a TV screen, while a group of African American students talk loudly in the back of the room. The movie is shut off abruptly, but it is hardly noticeable as the noise of the class escalates.

Please stop talking. The voice of the teacher is lost to laughter. *I will not accept this. Silence!* One girl in the back finally takes notice, and she turns around.

I don't have to listen to you, she tells the teacher loudly.

I am your teacher.

I don't give a damn if you are my teacher.

I already learned this. This is for your benefit. I already went to college, I don't know if you ever will. Now we are silent, and we wait to see how far he will go. He is a teacher not made for kids who bear the weight of their family's tears, who cannot listen to stories of white men who didn't need to cry. The girl stops, she didn't expect this, but she isn't surprised.

At least I ain't fat. She has nothing left to insult, she has been stripped of all power. She struggles to keep her face hard after another white man has reminded her of her insignificance. I hang my head as my teacher orders her out of the room.

The year ends, and I am left with moments such as these burning my memory, and little new knowledge of history or English. I cannot hold it all anymore, and now I am not sure the sacrifice of a conventional education is worth it. I cannot bear another year of watching teachers attempt and fail to reach out to kids who never learned how to be students in this educational system. Midway through high school, I have not yet heard a passionate teacher discuss a book. I'd like to have that experience, and the only way to get the one "good" English teacher for junior year is to join another program called Academic Choice.

◆ ◆ ◆

My English teacher sets his copy of *Stranger in the Village* by James Baldwin on his desk, and looks down at the cramped rows of mostly white faces below him.

I guess we can relate this story to ourselves, he tells us. I look around the room at the 18 Academic Choice kids with whom I spend most of my day. Many look up uneasily, waiting for our teacher to continue. We hope our too-quiet silence doesn't betray our discomfort. This teacher, however, expects such respect and attention because, as he often points out, we *chose* to be here.

Well, look around, he says. Then I notice that out of the five kids of color who ended up in this class by default of the computer, only one has shown up today. *Dennis?* he questions. Everyone now focuses on the one black kid, and I find myself waiting, defensively. *You are in a similar situation to the author of* Stranger in the Village. *How does it feel to be the only African American student in class?*

Dennis doesn't look around, hardly looks up, and responds quickly, *Fine.*

But do you ever feel uncomfortable? Is it hard for you?

It's fine. Dennis keeps his face flat, his hands on his desk, and I ache to change the subject. The too-quiet silence has intensified. I try to imagine staring out from Dennis's eyes onto a blur of well-intentioned white faces, and I watch my teacher intently, trying to decide if he realizes his mistake. I never expected such an intelligent and experienced teacher to cross this line, and I struggle to convince myself that he will never cause such humiliation again. We settle back into our normal attentive silence, and I attempt to concentrate on the story, and not on the reminder of what I have given up by joining this program.

I cannot seem to find the right balance between demanding academics and a broader education, and for the moment I have stopped searching for it in my classes. I sometimes think I have taken the easier way out. I have chosen hours of homework, high expectations, and no exceptions. Behind me, for now, I leave the work that so far has been too hard to finish, work that I must someday return to—to help dry history's tears from Patrice's face, and to sit in a class full of color, a rainbow of engaged students.

SKYLAR JAMES, a member of the class of 2006, is a student at Sonoma State University.

Late-Night Drives

Growing up was tough on my relationship with my father. He is a filmmaker, and worked late hours in San Francisco editing movies. In fact, the only time we really talked was when he would abandon his equipment to have a nice sit-down dinner with the family. And even then the attention was shared between my mother and brother. But, what I would always truly desire would be for him to tell me one of his world-famous stories. In those 10, maybe 15 minutes, all was right in the world. In those short moments nothing was wrong in our relationship. But these stories were only rare treats in an otherwise bland relationship.

One night last summer, however, my father invited me to San Francisco to turn off some equipment. "So there I was, escaping from the burning barracks with the rest of my platoon," he said, with such fire in his lungs it startled me. "We had been hit in the middle of the night. One minute I was dreaming about canned peaches and sauce, the next, guys are screaming." He took a moment to read an advancing sign on the freeway. "It wasn't until I had made it out that I realized we were missing a man. Not just any man, no no no, we were missing our sergeant!"

I was instantly intrigued. My dad was delivering the story in such a way that it felt as if I were right next to him in Vietnam.

"'Where's Sergeant Jones?' I asked a nearby soldier. They said he was in the burning house, still sleeping. When I asked why they didn't wake him, you know what they said?" he asked me. I shook my head. "They said," he continued, "that he was a nigger, and they wouldn't stick their neck out for any nigger." My eyes opened a little wider at this remark. It had always been an unwritten rule in my family to never say "nigger."

"So I said, 'Hey! I'm a nigger, would you leave me?' None of those boys responded, which answered my question."

"So what happened next?" I asked. My dad just smiled briefly and glanced at me before saying, "I went into that barracks and dragged our sergeant out." He had said it so quickly I could not tell if he would elaborate. A few seconds went by before I asked him what I thought was an obvious question. "So . . . did you get a medal or something?"

"No," he replied. The fiery talk had vanished from his lips, and the excitement in his face turned to a calm, bitter expression. He sighed, "Sergeant Jones never reported what happened that night. In fact, he gave me the worst possible grunt work."

I was thoroughly confused. "Wow, I guess it wasn't worth it, then," I blurted out. The car made a sudden turn to the side of the street we were now on, and came to a stop. The lights of passing cars danced off our faces. It was so quiet I almost could hear our heartbeats thumping; mine in anticipation, his in preparation.

He turned to me and said, "Son, sometimes doing the right thing doesn't mean you get a trophy or recognition. Sometimes, doing the right thing just means you can sleep easier at night." The silence was reinstated. After a few minutes he gave me a pat on the shoulder, and a passing car's lights revealed his smile. My dad turned the motor back on, and we pulled back onto the street.

My father's stories have influenced me in two significant ways. First, he showed me that doing something good or brave shouldn't be solely for recognition. It should be about what is right, and how it can help others rather than just oneself. Secondly, he showed me why I want to become a writer—to share my stories and lessons, and perhaps help someone else sleep easy at night.

SONIA ABRAMS, a member of the Berkeley High class of 1999, graduated in 2003 from Lewis and Clark College and is now living in the Bay Area.

I Was Country When Country Wasn't Cool

It's 6 a.m. on a cool July morning in Taylorsville, California, a town that's only four blocks long. The rickety barn creaks above my head as I stand ankle-deep in horse manure, brushing the knots out of my favorite horse's mane. My friends back home in the city are curled up warm in their beds. They wonder why every summer I go to a place where I have to get up at the crack of dawn and wear muddy clothes to be a ranch hand. But I know why. I do it to feel the wet nose of a horse as it nuzzles my arm, begging for a treat. I do it because of the way I laugh as I try to keep up with the fast-paced line-dancing, and for the screams of excitement as the cowboy hangs on to the bull for dear life.

As I scoop horse dung, I stop to think of the day ahead of me. I've been working on a running ranch for two weeks, and today it's coming to an end. In just a couple of hours, I'll be in a van with other muddy campers on our way back to the real world. I had gone to camp expecting to make some friends and enjoy typical camp recreation. But working in such an intense environment, close to animals, I soon discovered the commitment it takes to care for cows, horses, goats, and pigs. As a small girl I was always digging up salamanders in the garden, running to pet new dogs tied up outside of stores, and trying to identify a bug we recently captured in the backyard. My work on the ranch made my real interests come alive.

I live in Berkeley, California, a city known as one of the most diverse and bizarre places in the country. People in Berkeley are accepting of everything: races, cultures, sexualities, clothing, music. My closest friends listen to almost every kind of music: rap, hip-hop, swing, salsa, ska, alternative, and reggae.

So when I came home from living on a ranch with a passion for country music and ranch animals, I assumed my friends would be open to the new culture. Little did I realize that Berkeley is not the place for country bumpkins. Berkeley may have a lot of great crazes, but boot-stomping, bull-riding, and stall-mucking aren't among them. These are the essential ingredients that make up what I love in country life.

All my life, country music has been a big influence. I was seven years old when I decided to play the violin. Instead of playing classical music, like most other young violin players, I was drawn to bluegrass and klezmer. I loved how quick it was and how my fingers flew across the strings like they were dancing. At first, I played small gatherings and little coffee houses. At age 12, my group performed in front of 1,600 people. It made me happy to see people clapping, smiling, and dancing to the music. Most people don't realize that violin and fiddle are actually the same instrument. My friends try to picture me with a violin. They think of old men in tuxedos and powdered wigs playing Bach in front of stuffy old women. On the contrary, bluegrass music is jumping and dancing, people hooting and hollering from the audience.

I've tried to convince my city friends to give country music a try, but it's no use. However, my attempts have produced some surprising reactions. Recently, I was driving with a friend of mine, and I had the radio tuned to the one country station you can pick up in Berkeley. He refused to even listen, and without any warning tried to jump out of my car!

Country lifestyle is one thing I'm on my own about. I have to listen to country in my bedroom and go to the rodeo with only my camp friends. By discovering my friends' closed-mindedness, I have learned a lot about myself. I never thought of giving up my taste for something different, so I had to learn how to branch out and pursue my own passion. This has influenced my academic interests as well. My interest in biology and my decision to pursue a pre-veterinary program have been my own. The colleges I am applying to are determined by this passion and not by where my friends plan to go. I also have a new respect for the myriad directions my friends are choosing. I've learned that although it can be awkward and lonely to cut out on my own, it is worth it. I don't have to conform to what everyone else likes, so I'm free to show my individuality. I can learn more about who I am and who other people are. Now, it's fun to have something unique: something only I appreciate. I realize this is where open-mindedness begins.

TING W. HUNG graduated in the class of 2002 and attended UC San Diego.

My father and I once again stood at the arrival lounge at the airport on a hot summer night, waiting for my mother's arrival from Hong Kong. It was six months since we last saw her at the departure end of the same airport. This would be one of her two visits to us this year, her second visit would be in the Christmas time during her winter vacation. Her visit this time would be about three weeks, as usual in her past visits to us, then she would have to go back to her career as a violinist in Hong Kong. Since my father and I moved to the United States six years ago from Hong Kong, my mother and I have been living in two separate worlds that are bridged by long-distance calls and her regular visits to the United States.

The exit doors swung open, and passengers began flooding out of Customs, many of them searching very anxiously for their loved ones and hugging them out of overflow of emotion. But my father and I, we were very casual. After all, we had been to the lounge so many times to pick up my mother that all this had become routine. I stood very calmly; I felt no thrill seeing my mother at that moment, even though we had not seen each other in such a long time. Maybe it was because we have not lived together in such a long time that my impression of her had slowly faded. Then, she came out of the exit; we approached her, carried her luggage, and drove home.

For three weeks she stays and lives with us in the apartment that for most of the year is occupied only by my father and me. The first few days of her visits are often the hardest time to live through, the transition from the absence of someone very close to the immediate presence of that someone returning into my life. I live so independently on my own when my mother is away, even though we stay connected weekly through the phone, I always feel distant to her when she comes because of the time missing in our relationships. The gap between us always takes some time to shorten. But once I have adjusted to the addition to our life, I'd find my mother once again is "my mother." Despite my permanent relationship with my father, there are holes within me that only my mother can fill. She offers me help and advice about school and other decisions and I passionately accept her help. Whenever I'm stressed out about schoolwork, especially in the subject of English and writing, she is the first that I go to even though she can't even understand English. I go to her because she offers me encouragement and motivation. She was the one who talked me into trying out for sports, encouraging me to go for badminton because it fit into our Chinese cultural heritage. Gradually, we forget all our differences and we live as if we've never been separated. I feel motivated just by her presence; knowing that there's someone supporting me. All her words have made me a healthier person, both physically and mentally, my schoolwork improves, I'm more attentive and interested in a lot of different activities, and I'd feel very positive about almost anything.

Time goes by very fast, the three weeks are up, and back to the airport where it began. She goes back to her life and we go on with our own, my father and I. We know that she'll be back in the winter time, but for me, it gets to be very difficult to handle the adjustment within; from living so independently from my mother for most of the time, to feeling her existence in my life and then going back to living without her presence. The long-distance relationships between us, and all the toss-ups of feelings that I have, are hard to go through once every six months. The contrast between loneliness and hardship, encouragement and love, shape and reshape my character. Having all these experiences has made my values grow stronger and more mature, I grow more upon every one of her visits, and I am influenced by her words even after her departure. Every time I watch her go away at the airport, I always remind myself about all her encouragement and advice that will stay, even though physically an ocean separates us.

WHITNEY SMITH graduated from Berkeley High School in 1997. She attended Brown University and is currently a medical student at UC Davis.

STANFORD UNIVERSITY PROMPT

Attach a small photograph of something important to you and explain its significance. (Whitney submitted pictures of her two grandmothers, taken when they were teenagers.)

Short but mighty women have a long tradition in my family. At five-two, I am eye-level with the two impressive women who are my grand-mothers. Despite their common height, they are as different as can be. From them I inherit not only my size but the personality to back it up.

My maternal grandmother uses whatever tool she has on hand to accomplish the task before her; she has been known to butter bread with a butcher knife. She moved to Brazil when she was 29. She had never left the United States before, didn't speak a word of Portuguese, and had two small children. Undaunted, she threw herself into the ad-venture. After Brazil, she moved to Iran, visited communist Russia, and was a librarian in Papua New Guinea. (One of my Halloween costumes included a genuine grass skirt!) When she moved to California, I was seven years old. Though finished with traveling, she did not become a conventional grandmother. With Grandma, I danced in the San Fran-cisco Carnaval Parade (she loved it) and passed through the portals of Victoria's Secret for the first time. (She put down her foot at the purple satin bra—"What would your father say?") The importance of a well-fitting white shirt and a good book are among her legacies to me.

Mummers, my father's mother, has lived on the same street, just two blocks from her parents' home, since she married the boy next door more than 60 years ago. I live just around the corner and visit her often. She has taught me many things: to embroider, to stew spiced cherries, and, most important, to listen. A visit to Mummers never fails to include sitting at her kitchen table with a plate of gingersnaps. I've watched her put visitors at ease with well-worded questions designed to draw out personal interests. She is a traditionalist who appreciates orderliness but is not rigid in her thinking. She truly learns from the people around her, and they love her for it. She is willing to always listen to me, but I have discovered that it is I who can learn from her. Whether the subject be my friends, her childhood, the National Organization for Women, or religion, her insight and knowledge have helped me form my own opinions. In additional to all of her grace, she has, at 82, conquered Windows 95 and e-mail.

As I've grown older, I've discovered that aspects of my two grandmothers' personalities are fused in me. Like Grandma, I throw my entire self into whatever activity lies at hand. Sophomore year, I became the managing editor of the school paper. My job description was summed up in two sentences by the editor-in-chief. "You make sure the advertisements make it into the paper and call the printer. I don't really know what else you do." Left on my own, I looked around to see where I could be helpful. Two years later, my job has expanded to include a multitude of tasks. I spend so many hours at school that even the janitors say hi to me. I am in charge of printing, circulation, and advertising. I attend PTSA meetings, Back to School Night, and eighth-grade outreach events to expose parents to the paper. I write thank-you letters for donations and telephone patrons not receiving the paper. I run the business staff. Like Mummers, I listen to other people and help when I can. When an editor's page is lost on the computer, I comfort and help them. When a writer is having trouble with a story, I help them find someone to interview. Although I am now a veteran on the paper, I never stop listening to others, incorporating their ideas and learning from them.

It is from Grandma and Mummers that I inherit my determination, cheerfulness, value of education, and, above all, love of family. I am, however, my own person. No one else laughs as hard at themselves as I do. No one else loves organizing trips to the beach in the middle of the winter. No one else would venture to Paris by themselves and return with only one souvenir—a pair of three-inch cork platform shoes (to bolster my height, of course).

In Memoriam: Yonas Mehari

By Brenda Kahn, Essay Reader

Over Thanksgiving break in the fall of 2006, I spent some time thinking about Yonas Mehari, a senior at Berkeley High and one of the early-morning regulars at the essay readers' table in the College and Career Center. As one of the readers, I had gotten to know Yonas and had been charmed by his infectious smile and his upbeat nature despite a life of hardship and dislocation, and I felt invested in his success. He had one of the short UC essays under control—he had written about his leadership role with the Earphone Club—and now was working on the long essay. At first he was at a loss as to what to write about, but as he told me bits and pieces of his life, we had an "Aha!" moment: Clearly, he had a lot of material in his story of persecution as an ethnic Eritrean growing up in Ethiopia, the deportation of his family (which included eight children) to neighboring Eritrea, and ultimately their migration to the United States and the East Bay by way of Asmara, Yemen, and Germany.

I had plenty of time to mull over Yonas's stream-of-consciousness first draft during my Thanksgiving car trip to the Los Angeles area. By the time he was 10, he had witnessed unspeakable horrors and experienced devastating losses, including the death of his father from a respiratory infection that likely would have been minor here, but was fatal due to poverty and lack of medical care. He ended the essay on a positive note, by discussing his leadership role in creating the Ethiopian-Eritrean Student Union at Berkeley High. "Some people don't know where I come from," he wrote. "That is why I want to bring people together by starting a club for Ethiopian and Eritrean students that also includes other students, to help educate them and help them understand each other, and bring peace between them. I understand the importance of diversity. It's no longer abstract, but alive."

His physical and internal journey made for a compelling story, but Yonas was still struggling with written English, which he had only started to learn a few short years before. He was also struggling to get time on the computers at school to complete his UC essays and finish the online UC application, since his family didn't have the luxury of an Internet connection at home. While he was gleeful when he was chosen for the varsity BHS soccer team, it meant even less time to work on his essays and applications. Yonas's dream was to go to UC Berkeley and ultimately to study medicine (a goal solidified by a summer internship at Kaiser Hospital), but on that Thanksgiving weekend, I knew it would take a minor miracle to get the application done by the November 30 UC deadline.

That deadline was looming in my mind as the holiday break drew to a close, and I arrived back home with my family. But I was soon to discover that events had overtaken us. Sunday night I got a call with shocking news: Yonas had been murdered on Thanksgiving Day, along with his mother and older sister. Not on the streets of North Oakland, where he lived, and not by hoodlums, but gunned down in his family's apartment in a blaze of violence apparently stemming from a family feud. As I struggled to absorb the loss of this beautiful and promising 17-year-old, a scene from Yonas's essay-in-progress immediately came into focus, in which he had come within an inch of being killed when soldiers near the Eritrean border had machine-gunned a busload of refugees. Yonas survived a hail of bullets in that war-torn slice of East Africa only to be shot in the haven of the Bay Area, and by members of his extended family.

According to one of his brothers who survived the attack, Yonas was working on his college essays when the gunmen burst in. He had just finished writing these words, "I have had a very strict mother who always said study and study until we got tired of hearing it. Also she was one of the best mothers that I can imagine anyone having. Even neighbors used to pray and wish she was their mother."

The next morning, a table in the College and Career Center became a makeshift shrine as dozens of students dropped by to mourn the loss of their friend, and pay him tribute with flowers and messages scrawled on a large piece of paper. It turned out that Yonas had deeply touched many people in the Berkeley High community, both among the students and staff. And while I thought of him as my special project, I found out that several of the other college-essay readers knew him well, and were as fond of him as I was, and also had been rooting for him. The Bay Area's Eritrean community turned out in force for the three victims' service at the Greek Orthodox Cathedral in Oakland, which drew a standing-room-only crowd in excess of 1,000 mourners. We'll never know where Yonas's riveting long essay, intelligence, and drive would have taken him. What we do know is that he had a profound impact on his fellow English-language learners, as shown by the short essay below, which could have worked for any of the three UC essay prompts.

YONAS MEHARI was a member of the class of 2007. He was killed on November 23, 2006.

Earphone Club

Being an immigrant, it was hard for me to learn to speak and read in English. I did not read English in Ethiopia. In fact, I barely read even my own language, Amharic, because of the poor quality of the schools. I have been in the Earphone Club for the last four years. The club is mostly to help English learners get into the habit of reading in English or in their native language by listening to a book on tape while following along in a book. The club taught me to love reading. Because of this positive experience, I recruited my friends into the club, which landed me in a leadership role. I was elected the vice president of the club in my sophomore year, a position I've held ever since. My responsibilities are to organize and plan meetings, e-mail people to remind them when the meetings are, and run the club when the president is absent. I also continue to recruit new members. Today, I don't really need the headphones to read, but I still go there every Wednesday to help others who are in the same situation as I was.

Acknowledgments

First, a thank you to Berkeley High School Vice Principal Rory Bled, who as the college advisor many years ago welcomed writers, that is "readers," to the College Center.

Many thanks to Rick Ayers, founder and lead teacher of Communication Arts and Science, a small school at Berkeley High, who was instrumental in pushing this book along.

Thank you to Vicky Elliott, who helped with the selecting, editing, and production of this collection, both editions! Thank you to Suzanne Chun, who designed the original edition (*True Admissions*).

Thank you to Kris Seeman and Tami Uecker, both of whom helped collect essays, and Julie Owen, who helped with selecting. Thank you to Ellie Smith, who provided excellent second opinions second-go-round. And thank you to the English teachers of Berkeley High for laying the essay-writing groundwork for students.

Also thanks to my son, Nat Smith, who did a very good job badgering his friends to send me their essays, and to the untold parents who pushed their kids into doing the same.

And of course, this book could not have been completed without the help and support of Ilene Abrams, Berkeley High School's college advisor, who manages to give excellent and personal advice to hundreds of students, and our most gracious Edna Harris, who runs the College and Career Center's day-to-day operation.

There are two other groups who deserve very special thanks: Over the years, many who use writing in their professional life have volunteered to be essay readers for Berkeley High. I wish I had all their names, but I don't. However, incomplete though the list is, I would like to gratefully acknowledge Jane Adams, Linda Artel, Laurie Bronson, Clair Brown, Vicky Elliott, Cheryl Fragiadakis, Sally Hopkins, Abby Ginsburg, Reka Goode, Carrie Horsey, Brenda Kahn, Jamie Keller, Rachel Kimball, Vicki Laden, Henry Mayer, Wendy Morrison, Betsy Partridge, Angela Price, Joanne Reichert, Winifred Reilly, Hilary Roberts, Ellen Singer-Vine, Catherine Stern, Tami Uecker, and Jim Walker, all of whom generously gave of their time over the last four years to help guide untold numbers of students on the path to higher education.

And finally, what would this be without the students of Berkeley High, who donated their essays to this project? Simply put, they are the best.

Thank you, all.

JANET HUSEBY